TRAVEL DIARIES
OF A NATURALIST

Peter Scott

TRAVEL DIARIES OF A NATURALIST

III

JAPAN   INDONESIA   HONG KONG   CHINA
MONGOLIA   THE PHILIPPINES   MALAYSIA
AUSTRALIA   NEW ZEALAND

Edited by Miranda Weston–Smith
Photographs by Philippa Scott

COLLINS
8 Grafton Street, London W1
1987

*To all those who have worked
to protect the beauty and wonder of nature,
and to those who have made it possible for me
to travel and to enjoy that beauty and wonder
in so many different parts of the world.*

William Collins Sons & Co Ltd
London · Glasgow · Sydney · Auckland
Toronto · Johannesburg

BRITISH LIBRARY CATALOGUING IN PUBLICATION DATA

Scott, *Sir*, Peter, *1909–*
Travel diaries of a naturalist.
3
1. Scott, *Sir*, Peter, *1909–*   2. Ornithologists
—Great Britain—Biography
I. Title   II. Weston-Smith, Miranda
598′.092′4   SK17.S27

ISBN 0–00–217707–2

First published 1987
© Peter Scott 1987

Maps by Brian and Gill Lloyd

Filmset by Ace Filmsetting Ltd, Frome
Colour and black and white reproduction by
Alpha Reprographics Ltd, Harefield
Made and printed in Great Britain by
William Collins Sons and Co Ltd, Glasgow

Contents

Acknowledgements

The journeys and the production of this book have been made possible by the collaboration and generous help of a large number of people. We would like to give special thanks to: Jane Bere, Martin Bragg and Barry Highland, the Chinese Department and the Map Department of Cambridge University Library, Crispin Fisher, Anne Harding, IUCN, IWRB, Lars Eric Lindblad and Lindblad Travel, Nancy Nash, Carol O'Brien, Cassandra Phillips, Ken and Sue Searle, Ron and Valerie Taylor, the Wildfowl Trust, WWF Hong Kong, WWF International, WWF Malaysia.

PS
M W-S
May 1986

Editor's Note

This third volume of Sir Peter Scott's travel diaries contains even more facsimile material than the earlier books, in keeping with his wish that the published diaries should retain as much as possible of their original character. As a result the quantity of printed narration has been reduced to make room for a stronger notebook atmosphere. *Travel Diaries of a Naturalist III* contains entries and drawings from 8 out of 65 of Sir Peter's travel diaries; Volume I drew from 15 diaries, and Volume II from 13.

I have, as before, introduced maps showing where Sir Peter and Lady Scott travelled and Sir Peter has added some material to his original notes; these passages are indented in the text. He has also added the footnotes. Words or phrases enclosed in square brackets have been inserted by me.

Italics have been used to distinguish scientific from vernacular names of animals and plants as well as for their normal purposes. Only the species names of animals begin with capital letters, other more general ones do not. For example a Whooper Swan, but a swan; a Long-legged Buzzard is the name of a species of bird, a white-headed buzzard is not.

The Pinyin system for the transliteration of Chinese characters in to the Western alphabet is now widely adopted (in preference to the older Wade-Giles method) and this is the one used in this book. It has not been adhered to rigidly, however, and so old Canton is usually called Kwangchow (not the Pinyin Guangzhou), and as the capital of China is well known both as Peking and Beijing these departures from Pinyin have – like some other irregularities in Sir Peter's style – been left unaltered.

The reader may find the following list of acronyms helpful:

CITES	Convention on International Trade in Endangered Species
CSIRO	Commonwealth Scientific and Industrial Research Organization
EPO	Environmental Protection Office
FAO	Food and Agricultural Organization of the United Nations
IUCN	International Union for Conservation of Nature and Natural Resources
IWRB	International Waterfowl Research Bureau
NGO	Non-governmental organization
PRC	People's Republic of China
RSPB	Royal Society for the Protection of Birds

SSC   Species Survival Commission of IUCN formerly Survival
Service Commission

UNEP   United Nations Environment Programme

UNESCO United Nations Educational, Scientific and Cultural
Organization

WWF   World Wildlife Fund (recently renamed World Wildlife
Fund for Nature)

The illustrations have been reproduced from Sir Peter's diaries
most of which measure 15.5×22 cm. It has been necessary to
reduce some and magnify others.

M W-S

May 1986

Introduction

How many readers of this book may have seen, or remember, the earlier volumes of my travel diaries I do not know but, at the risk of repetition, I must tell you that for as long as I can remember I have been a naturalist with a perpetual itch to show wild nature to other people in the hope that they too will get as much delight from it as I have done. And the more people who become interested in the natural world and committed to it, the greater the chance that wild nature will continue to exist.

The travels which make up this volume had various different objectives. The first journey, described in Chapter 1, was made in our familiar and much-loved ship the *Lindblad Explorer* from Japan, by way of the Pacific islands, to Bali in 1976. I was travelling as one of the ship's naturalists and lecturers, at the invitation of our long-time friend, Lars Eric Lindblad.

Then, in Chapter 2, comes our first visit to China and Mongolia in 1978 on a Lindblad land tour for which, once more, I was the naturalist. There followed another expedition in the *Lindblad Explorer* (Chapter 3) to the Philippines, and thereafter to Sabah in Malaysia to see the Orangutans.

In the following year (Chapter 4) I went on a whistle-stop tour of Australia to launch the World Wildlife Fund there, closely followed by a short spell in Malaysia to introduce and make the commentary for a film that was being made for WWF Malaysia.

In the same year I went again to China with WWF colleagues to establish a firm conservation link and get a programme going for the Giant Panda (Chapter 5). After completing our WWF business in Beijing we were taken on a field trip to the Everwhite Mountain, in the north-east corner of the country, where there were reputed still to be tigers. When we got there we found they had not seen any for some years. But, far out on a great reservoir, we saw three ducks which *may* have been Scaly-sided [Chinese] Mergansers.

In 1980 we went to an IWRB Waterfowl Conference in Japan (Chapter 6) and saw great numbers of wintering Whooper Swans in a salt-water bay. From Japan I went on alone to launch the World Conservation Strategy – an international document which was drawn up by IUCN in collaboration with WWF, UNEP, UNESCO and FAO – in Peking and Hong Kong.

In the autumn of the same year we went with the great American zoologist, George Schaller, to select a place for a Giant Panda Research Centre in the Wolong Reserve, in the western Chinese province of Sichuan (Chapter 7).

The last chapter describes a visit to Hong Kong in order to advise on the development of the wonderful Mai Po Marshes as a reserve, with strong educational overtones, based on the techniques we have developed at the Wildfowl Trust.

My wife and I will always be infinitely grateful to all the people who made these exciting journeys possible for us.

Diademichthys
lineatus

Peter Scott.

Torishima 8 August 1976

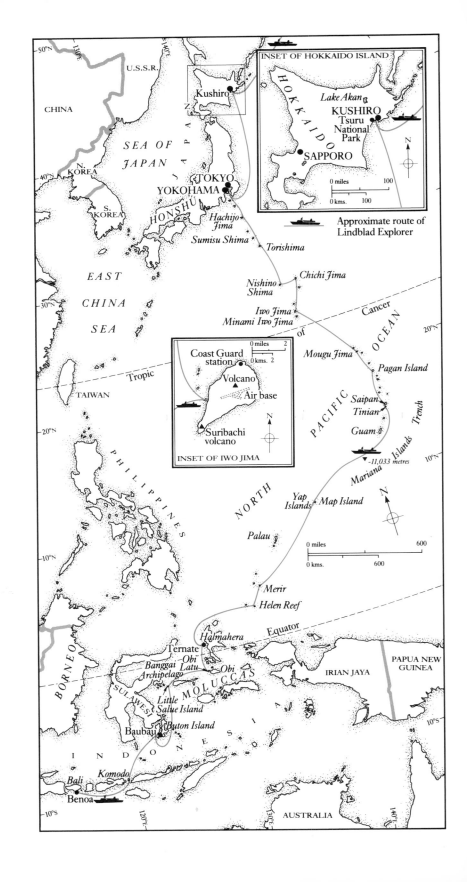

50°N

130°

140°

U.S.S.R.

CHINA

INSET OF HOKKAIDO ISLAND

HOKKAIDO

Lake Akan

Kushiro

KUSHIRO
Tsuru
National
Park

SAPPORO

0 miles   100

0 kms.   100

N

SEA OF
JAPAN

40°N

N.
KOREA

S.
KOREA

HONSHU

TOKYO
YOKOHAMA

Hachijo
Jima

Sumisu Shima

Torishima

Approximate route of
Lindblad Explorer

EAST

CHINA

SEA

30°N

Nishino
Shima

Chichi Jima

Iwo Jima
Minami Iwo Jima

Cancer

of

OCEAN

20°N

TAIWAN

Tropic

0 miles   2

0 kms.   2

Coast Guard
station

Volcano

Air base

Suribachi
volcano

N

INSET OF IWO JIMA

Mougu Jima

Pagan Island

Saipan
Tinian

Guam

-11,033 metres

PACIFIC

Mariana Islands Trench

10°N

20°N

PHILIPPINES

NORTH

Yap
Islands

Map Island

Palau

0 miles   600

0 kms.   600

N

10°N

Merir

Helen Reef

Equator

BORNEO

Halmahera

Ternate

Obi
Latu

Obi

Banggai
Archipelago

MOLUCCAS

IRIAN JAYA

PAPUA NEW
GUINEA

SULAWESI

Little
Salue Island

Buton Island

INDONESIA

Baubau

10°S

Bali

Komodo

Benoa

120°E

130°E

140°E

AUSTRALIA

10°S

CHAPTER 1

From Japan to Bali in the
Lindblad Explorer

DIARIES 25 AND 26 1976

In the summer of 1976 Philippa and I made a fantastic voyage through the Pacific Ocean, travelling in the *Lindblad Explorer*, on which I was staff naturalist and lecturer. We went on board at Prince Rupert, British Columbia, heading northward to Alaska and the Bering Sea. Having pushed up as far as the sea ice we then turned south via the Aleutians to Japan where the passengers disembarked and a new group joined the ship for the voyage through the Japanese islands, the Bonins, the Marianas, Yap, Palau, Halmahera, Sulawesi and Komodo to Bali – whence we returned home. We had been eight weeks in the 'little red ship' starting from Canada, crossing the Arctic Circle, and heading south via Japan to cross the equator in Indonesia – a journey of some 11,000 miles.

The northern cruise in Canada and Alaska was recorded in a diary that appeared as Chapter Five in *Travel Diaries of a Naturalist II*.

The first half of our voyage ended in Yokohama but before we reached it we went to the northern island of Hokkaido on . . .

TUESDAY 3 AUGUST 1976
By 0900 we were travelling by bus out of Kushiro. The first stop was about 15 miles out of town – the Tsuru National Park (Tsuru = crane). It is evidently an important tourist attraction. Several buses and twenty or thirty cars were in the car park at 1000. We were, of course, especially interested in the place because, in the field of cranes, it has very similar objectives to our Wildfowl Trust.

In the park there are apparently 18 adult cranes in captivity, and breeding. In winter they attract large numbers of migratory Japanese (Manchurian) Cranes – some from wild breeding areas in Japan but mostly from Manchuria. Up to 250 now come; a few years back there were only about 100.

The breeding pens were nice and large – about 40 yards wide and maybe 200 yards long – and inside was natural marshy grass with small pools and water-supply ditches. It looked very attractive though the 15-foot wire netting was unsightly. Small willow bushes and birch trees were growing in a haphazard distribution about the pens. About five pairs were in the large pens. In addition there were

Grus japonensis

Japanese Crane, *Grus japonensis*, Hokkaido

four immature birds in very small independent cages and near the main gate three brown birds which I took to be this year's young. One bird flew in and was loudly greeted by one of the breeding pairs; I presumed this to be a wild one.

Later in the day we went on a boat trip on Lake Akan to see the Ball Alga called 'Marimo' (it looks like green tennis balls). The boat was a crowded passenger steamer and there was a continuous commentary by a Japanese girl who sometimes broke into song (a considerable relief!).

On the way back from the algae we saw four Eastern Goosanders – my first view, I thought, of *Mergus merganser orientalis*. The subspecies is slightly smaller but not distinguishable in the field and, on looking it up later, I discovered that we must have been looking at *Mergus merganser merganser* – the same Goosander race as we have in Europe, whose breeding range extends across Europe and Asia to the Pacific and which winters in Japan. *M. m. orientalis* breeds in Afghanistan, Tibet and Turkestan, and winters in India, Burma and western China. It has not been recorded from Japan. Black mark, Scott!

We had good views of the Japanese Pied Kingfisher at Lake Akan.

Lunch in a nice restaurant at Akan and afterwards a walk round the Ainu village. No pure hairy Ainu were to be seen, but the shops in a steep street were amusing and decorative.

And so to sea again in the *Lindblad Explorer* bound for Yokohama, after a dance on the quay and a speech by the mayor.

Japanese Pied Kingfisher
Ceryle lugubris lugubris

Truck driver.... — NICKY

From 1812 for several years Michael Faraday, the discoverer of electricity, gave lectures at the Royal Institute in London. He once said: "The lecturer should give the audience full reason to believe that <u>all</u> his powers have been exerted for their pleasure and instruction.

WHY DO I BELIEVE IN NESSIE?

Although ~~I've~~ Phil & I have <u>watched</u> the surface of the loch for long periods & I have twice <u>dived</u> in it, we've never <u>seen</u> one of the animals ~~myself~~ ourselves.

But we've been interested in the subject for nearly 20 years.

As I ~~have~~ told you, I think, I am a <u>painter</u> by <u>profession</u> ~~and~~ but I'm also a <u>biologist</u> by <u>training</u>. And a <u>naturalist</u> by inclination as well.

I like to think I have an open mind.
Or at least <u>half</u> open.   Like the
Irish railway crossing keeper...... who was half expecting a train

I find that after dismissing the <u>hoaxes</u>, the deliberate <u>falsehoods</u>, the <u>hallucinations</u>, the <u>misidentifications</u> and the <u>honest errors</u>,

THERE REMAINS A HARD CORE OF EVIDENCE WHICH CANNOT BE EXPLAINED IN TERMS OF KNOWN PHENOMENA OR ATTRIBUTED TO KNOWN SPECIES OF LIVING ANIMALS.

So I think there's something <u>there</u> that deserves further study.

I'm <u>appalled</u> by the attitude of <u>some</u> scientists who are <u>afraid</u> to study the Loch Ness phenomena because it might damage their <u>reputation</u>.

SCIENCE IS ABOUT <u>FINDING THE TRUTH</u> — <u>NOT ABOUT REPUTATIONS</u>, and whether or not you will be elected to this or that learned society.

I'm <u>appalled</u> that a young scientist should have lost his job with our leading museum in London at least in <u>part</u> because he studied the Loch Ness evidence. "Taking the night tram to Inverness"

I'm <u>also appalled</u> that a great many reputable people, who've <u>seen</u> what they are <u>convinced</u> are large animals in Loch Ness, don't dare to <u>talk</u> about it for fear of <u>ridicule</u>.

That is <u>not</u> a <u>healthy</u> situation.

The first recorded sighting was by St Columba in the 6th Century A.D. 565. Since then There've been several thousand documented sightings, culminating in the recent photographs coupled with sonar — underwater echo-location.

I know that the mind can only absorb what the seat can endure. So I will try to be brief.

WEDNESDAY 4 AUGUST

At sea between Kushiro and Yokohama.

On the last leg of the first cruise we have had several days at sea and various entertainments have been devised for the amusement of the passengers. I have been required to recite my party pieces – 'The Hunting of the Snark' and Milne's 'The Knight whose armour didn't squeak'.

We had some acting games too, and I was set to mime a lady getting undressed and getting into bed. I got a good laugh by taking off imaginary panties and picking them up off the floor with my toe.

THURSDAY 5 AUGUST

Arrived in Yokohama. Ryozo Kakizawa, who is working on swan behaviour using bill patterns of Whoopers at Hyoko, came on board to talk. With him was Tsutomo Suzuki, Secretary of the Kanagawa Branch of the Wild Bird Society of Japan. Kakizawa knew all about our swan work and about Dafila [Scott] by name. We liked him very much. That evening I bought a camera for Phil which is to be my silver wedding present to her in two days' time.

A _Graphium_
drinking

FRIDAY 6 AUGUST

A day of considerable pressure. Passport photos for the Indonesian visas we shall need later on the cruise. Mail from home. Then the train from Yokohama to Tokyo where we were met by Stewart Jack from the British Embassy in the white Rolls Royce. Lunch with HE Sir Michael Wilford.

Two separate audiences – the first with HIH Prince Akihito [the Crown Prince] and the second with HIH Prince Hitachi [his younger brother]. The Crown Prince has a great interest in fishes and is very knowledgeable about them. He has a wall of aquaria in his study. Prince Hitachi is an ornithologist of distinction. Their father, the Emperor, has a deep interest in marine biology.

Phil bought a silver wedding present for me – a beautiful silk shirt with an elegant Japanese pattern and birds on it.

We made our return trip to Yokohama by train in the 'rush hour' and arrived back at the ship with six minutes to spare before sailing time, having run all the way from the station to the dock. Delaying the ship's departure is something that staff members must _never_ do. It would have made the Captain very cross, so the return train journey caused us considerable anxiety.

We were delighted to find on board our great friends Ron and Valerie Taylor who are travelling with us to Bali. They are the famous Australian underwater camera-team who shot many of the sequences in _Blue Water White Death_ and _Jaws_.

SATURDAY 7 AUGUST

We landed at a Japanese island called Hachijo Jima which has a population of 11,000 on 19,000 acres. I wrote down the 10 bird species that I positively identified – and 4 fish species which the anglers on the pier had caught. I also saw 3 different species of butterflies and 2 dragonflies, and heard some tree frogs peeping. The island has a Folk Museum which was rather well done.

It was our Silver Wedding Anniversary and we had a celebratory dinner with our special friends – Hasse Nilsson (the Captain) and his wife Ammi, Soames Summerhays and François Gohier – both fellow staff members. I think Phil enjoyed the evening as much as I did. How can anyone be so lucky as me? I echo Petronius Arbiter, 'Yes I have lived. Never can unkind fate take what was given in that earlier hour.' It was a very happy dinner party.

Bonin Petrel

SUNDAY 8 AUGUST

In the morning we passed a pinnacle rock called Sumisu Shima which had lots of Brown Boobies, Noddy and Sooty Terns. At sea we identified the Bonin Gadfly Petrel as well as Wedge-tailed Shearwaters (*Puffinus pacificus chlororhynchus*). Then we came to Torishima, a steep volcanic island which is the only nesting place of Steller's Albatross – *Diomedea albatrus* – one of the most endangered bird species in the world. The colony consists of 20 to 30 pairs and the total population is estimated at 150 birds. At this time of year we saw none, but we did see a rat which may be one of the causes of the birds' rarity, though the volcano is a more probable reason.

Phil was apparently the first woman to land on Torishima where the volcano is still active. To the consternation of our Japanese

The summit of Torishima which was still steaming

*Oplegnathus
punctatus.*

guide, a small party which included Phil climbed up to the steaming sulphurous area near the top of the island. But they came to no harm. Later we had our first goggling in Japanese waters, which included some interesting new fish species including two species of morwong (*Goniistus zebra* and *G. zonatus*) and a butterfly fish (*Chaetodon daedelma*) which I had never seen before.

I drew a couple of the plants that were growing above the beach.

MONDAY 9 AUGUST

Noon: Nishino Shima. These are small low islands. There had been an eruption three years ago, and a new island came up, which eventually joined on to the first. We telegraphed for permission to land and were told not to on any account as a survey was due to start shortly. Brown Boobies had 7 week-old young. We sailed on immediately.

TUESDAY 10 AUGUST

Chichi Jima. Before breakfast: goggling. An uninteresting place, with some swell. Some beginners tried out their snorkelling gear, but it was a very poor start for them. After breakfast: more goggling. A much better place with outstanding diversity of fishes and a lot of coral species.

Hideharu Takigawa, who left the ship today, gave me some books on Torishima. He was very nice, but kept calling me Dr Peterson! As I could not usually remember his name correctly we were quits!

Fish Ball. Something I have never seen before. This swarm of small fish, swimming very fast, passed by before I could see them properly. There must have been several hundred fish about 3 inches long and the egg shaped ball was about 3ft on its longest axis.

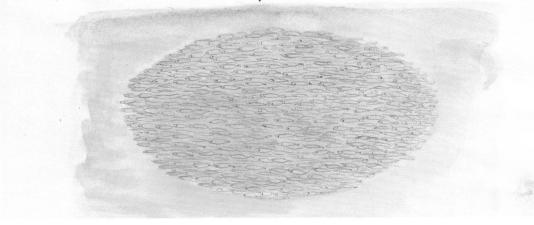

Chaetodon
  daedelma

Torishima 8/8
Chichi Jima 10/8

Goniistius zebra. Zebra Morwong.
  Goniistius = Cheilodactylus

Goniistius zonatus.
  Striped Morwong.

View from the road on Chichi Jima

Later I visited the Marine Research Station and sat getting names from *The Inshore Fishes of Japan* for nearly two hours. I found a great many of the fish species I have been seeing in the last two days. There is a curious satisfaction in being able to put a scientific name to a fish that you have just seen for the first time, or to confirm the name of one that you've seen before. I have been trying to think why this should be so. I think the answer must be that, as a naturalist, you always want to know more about any animal you see, and if you know its name you can read about it, you can compare it with related species, you can look out for the species which mimic it, and learn more about its distribution – and there is some point in recording its behaviour, its relative abundance, and its individual variation. There is, of course, also a certain satisfaction in being able to say to an obscure fish, 'Aha! I know you.'

In the evening our Cruise Director Lyall Watson gave an excellent lecture on the war in the Pacific in general, and on the part played in it by the island of Iwo Jima (which we shall visit tomorrow):

Japan in isolation after League of Nations' strictures. Anti-Comintern pact signed with Hitler. Sino-Japanese war 1937. 1939 – the Axis. Early German successes. Japanese need oil. Move towards Indonesia. Pre-emptive strike – Pearl Harbor December 1941. Capture of Philippines and South East Asia. Consolidated for two years. (Japanese rule so unpopular that colonialism was finished and the countries all became independent at the war's end.) Iwo

22

Jima needed as an air base for protecting US bombers on raids to Japan. At 0900 hours on 19 February 1945, after 72 days of continuous bombing, US landing. 30,000 men of 5th Marine Corps. 26 days to capture the island. 6,000 marines died. In all 26,000 people were killed. Iwo Jima became a base for saturation bombing of mainland Japan by US. March 1945 five raids. On one night 100,000 died in Tokyo. 6 August: Hiroshima. 9 August: Nagasaki. 14 August: surrender.

WEDNESDAY 11 AUGUST

Iwo Jima. Morning: one and a half miles to US Coast Guard HQ (40 men). I joined a party from the ship which went in Japanese trucks to the top of the Suribachi volcano and monuments. The memorials were not very beautiful to my eye, but the enormity of the death toll in the battle for the island and for Suribachi volcano in particular made being there an awful but moving experience.

Ron and Val Taylor didn't go ashore but took a zodiac out and spent the morning diving and snorkelling. I wished I had been with them, instead of sight-seeing on the battlefields.

But after the War Memorial on the hilltop I joined up with Phil for a walk along a beach to some hot springs and bubbling mud puddles which were quite impressive. Then back to the ship and on our way southward again.

In the afternoon we passed Little Iwo Jima (or Minami Iwo Jima). Thin wave clouds hung like a veil over the 3,181 foot volcano.

Fumarole on the beach on Iwo Jima

FRIDAY 13 AUGUST

Mougu Jima (Mariana Islands). The ship anchored in the middle of an old volcano about half a mile from the three steep islands of the crater rim. There were 3 species of boobies, 2 species of noddies, 2 species of tropic birds, Great Frigates, Fairy Terns, and king-fishers.

The snorkelling was very good. I recorded 98 species and with others brought it to well over the hundred in the day. Altogether a great day.

SATURDAY 14 AUGUST

Pagan Island. Landed with Lyall, Robbie Hernandez and John Green to prospect at a small village. Apparently there are about 75 people living on the island.

We walked along a track in *great heat* as far as a lagoon behind a beach, where we swam to cool off. A Top Minnow and a goby were there. Also a kingfisher and a dark phase Reef Heron.

An attractive island but very hot. The islanders apparently live by hunting and fishing. Some of them had been to an off-shore island and were just back with 51 dead flying foxes. A rat was seen on the island. Megapodes* are said to be fairly common still.

* Megapodes or mound-builders lay their eggs in huge mounds of rotting vegetation which provide the heat for incubation. When the compost heat is exhausted they scratch the top off the mound to allow the sun to complete the incubation.

Minami Iwo Jima as we left in the evening

Scarus ✗ lepidus
    ? tricolor.

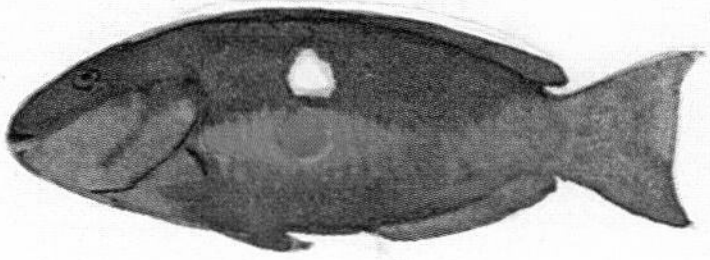

White

Blue

Green

Naso brevirostris

Chaetodon lunula

Bodianus axillaris

Acanthurus pyro·ferrus. orange opercular spot.

Holocentrus spiniferum

Pomacentrus sp
  Chromis sp

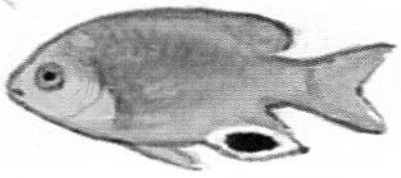

Apogon 5 lines black bed spot
   Paramia quinquelineata

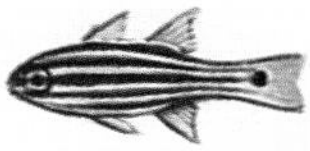

Chromis Green-brown. Blue eye & nose, yellow tail
   sp. anal & dorsal tip black with hyaline fringe.
     black axil spot.

Pterois antennata.

Myrolabrichthys tuka?
  all deep blue ♂

Caesio sp.
Pteracaesio
  tile

Grouper

Neocirrhites
armatus

Eleotrid
Pogonoculius ?
zebra ?

Chromis atripes?

Plagiotremus
rhynorhynchus

Labroides
dimidiatus ?
juvenile

Plectroglyphidodon
phoenixensis ??

SUNDAY 15 AUGUST

The connotations of World War II still almost totally overshadow the islands of Saipan and Tinian. They are a part of US history, and are still covered with evidence of the terrible things which happened on them – rusting wrecks in the lagoons, rusting tanks on shore and on the reefs, bunkers pock-marked with shell fire, Quansett buildings, airport runways, temporary harbours, and tourist maps giving the gruesome toll of US and Japanese lives.

There is an 833-foot cliff at the north end of Saipan over which hundreds of Japanese threw themselves in a massive communal suicide rather than be taken alive.

The capture of Saipan cost 3,144 American lives and 13,448 wounded.

200,000 American troops prepared for the invasion of Japan on Saipan, but the atom bombs that were dropped on Hiroshima and Nagasaki stopped the war before they set out. Ghastly as the Japanese casualties were, who knows how much greater the carnage might have been on both sides without the bombs.

Tinian. A bus took us to the airfield where the atom bombs were loaded for Hiroshima and Nagasaki. On the edge of the aircraft parking bays two plaques are mounted 100 yards apart. It took me back to the two raids over Germany which I made in August 1941 – to Keil and to Cologne; I remembered waiting on the tarmac to board the Stirling Bombers. And I visualized my friend Len Cheshire, who had been the British Observer for the Hiroshima raid, standing on the tarmac before take-off on that terrible mission which ended the Second World War.

Beside each plaque was a frangipani tree for death and a palm tree for life.

It was a peaceful sunny place which led directly to the holocaust in Japan, but which in turn may yet save us from World War III.

MONDAY 16 AUGUST

At sea over the deepest part of the ocean – a spot in the Mariana Islands trench that, at 11,033 metres, is nearly half as deep again as Everest is high (8,847 metres). The pressure at that depth is 7.7 tons per square inch. We had a joke ceremony of filling a time capsule with comical items and finally consigned a weighted paint drum to the depths. An hour later the passengers were reminded that the drum was reaching the bottom at about that time 11 kilometres (7 miles) down.

WEDNESDAY 18 AUGUST

Map Island in the Yap group. The village was *very beautiful* and the people friendly. They mostly chewed betel nut incessantly, but had a lovely relationship with their domestic animals. Dogs, pigs and chickens appeared to be integrated members of the family.

The men danced and sang sitting. The songs rather monotonous,

1976

<u>Tues. 17 August.</u> <u>Ulithi Atoll.</u> Caroline Islands.

a.m. <u>Mog.mog.</u> Rainstorms intermittent. Dances.
Delightful people.

Lesser Noddy <u>Anous tenuirostris</u>
Sooty Tern <u>Sterna fuscata</u>
Brown Booby <u>Sula leucogaster</u>
Black-naped Tern <u>Sterna sumatrana.</u>
Reef Heron (one white one dark phase) <u>Demigretta sacra.</u>
Ruddy Turnstone <u>Arenaria interpres</u>
Red-footed Booby. <u>Sula sula</u>
Microhesian Starling. <u>Aplonis opacus.</u>
Red-tailed Tropic Bird <u>Phaethon rubricauda</u>

Skink

Skink.

p.m. <u>Falalop.</u>

Naso tuberosus
Thalassoma fuscum sm
Thalassoma purpureum
   (= umbrostigma)

Thalassoma sp. quinquevittata
Thalassoma sp.
Thalassoma janseni

Rhinecanthus rectangulus.

Fodiator acutus. Sharp chinned Flying Fish

T. quinquevittata ♀

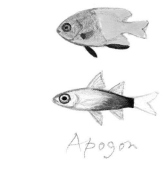

Apogon

Macropharyngodon
meleagris

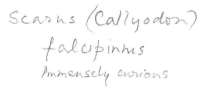

Scarus (Callyodon)
falupinus
Immensely curious

the whole scene full of colour. The topless girls also sat for their welcome songs but later with bamboo staves they danced more actively – a dance said to encourage the men to 'deeds of derring-do'. The backdrop was the famous Yapi stone money – huge round stones each with a hole in the middle – brought long ago (mostly) from Palau – but still evidently a basic banking system in the Yap Islands.

The aura of the village was happy and very peaceful. One wonders how much the pattern is influenced by the betel nut.

FRIDAY 20 AUGUST

Merir. Arrived midday. Two abortive attempts to anchor in the tide rip at the north end of the island. We finally went in on the east side. I snorkelled in to prospect a zodiac passage over the reef edge, which was achieved by all zodiacs – though some got rather wet. Birds: frigates, Fairy Terns, Black Noddies, two all-dark shearwaters and Common Sandpipers.

There is a single family living on Merir, though I did not meet them, the Antonio family which consists of Andres Antonio, wife Diane, 12-year-old son, and a baby born on the ship bringing them to the island, now called Dave Prince Antonio. Apparently they knew nothing of our arrival until Lyall touched the man's arm through the open window of his little house. Subsequently a good supply of foodstuffs was brought to them from the ship.

We missed meeting them because we were swimming on the outer reef outside the breakers where there were several female turtles and a few fish not seen in Palau yesterday, including my old friend *Ptereleotris tricolor*, a snapper new to me, *Lutjanus semicinctus*, and an exquisite *Anthias* with deep crimson (looking almost black) dorsal fin with the first spine held forward of vertical, yellow shoulders and elegant white pelvics. This may be *A. carberryi*, but also may not be. (*Mirolabrichthys dispar* actually.) There were also jumping tuna, sea snakes and a big Humphead Maori Wrasse.

SATURDAY 21 AUGUST

Helen Reef. One of the finest reef drop-offs on which I ever swam. When we entered the water a shoal of 100 large Humphead Parrot Fish came to see what kind of animals we were. I only saw two sharks – one dark with white eye and the other *Carcharinus albimarginatus* (the Ocean Whitetip). Phil saw a large Manta Ray underwater.

I had about an hour snorkelling, followed by three quarters of an hour SCUBA diving to 60 feet down the vertical cliff. Then more snorkelling.

It was a morning to remember.

SUNDAY 22 AUGUST

Ternate: entry port to Indonesia. Ashore for a bus ride to the old Sultan's palace, where there were dances and coconut milk in glasses and a hard octagonal biscuit. A pleasant walk back through the town. There were quantities of red parrots in the houses and shops; they were very tame and seemed to be in very good condition. This was the Chattering Lory, *Lorius garrulus garrulus*, a beautiful red bird with yellow 'wrists', a yellow patch on the upper back and dark blue wings – very noisy and talkative.

The town had a very pleasant feeling about it, although there were times when the pressure of people all round was a little overpowering. The fruit market was very nice, although the smell of

Merir Fishes.

Lutjanus semicinctus

Lutjanus gibbus

Ptereleotris evides

Glyphidodontpps p leucopomus

Bodianus sp
Cheilinus rhodochrus?

Mirolabrichthys dispar

Opposite: Dancers on Map Island, Yap Islands, Philippine Sea

29

Fishing boats at Ternate, Halmahera

Kuhliidae = Aloleholes

Kuhlia marginata
Kuhlia rupestris
K. Taeniura

Arothron

durians – a large spiny fruit – was extremely pervading and unpleasant.

We bought a lychee-like fruit called rambutan and a smaller smooth fruit with a sharper taste called lansat. We saw, but did not taste till later, mangosteen – a delicious fruit which seems to have some citrus connections – and salak or cobra fruit, which is nutty and dry, but with a very subtle flavour, and a skin like snakeskin.

At the foot of the dock wall opposite to the ship there was some quite colourful coral and I could see a few fish – the Black-banded Toby (*Canthigaster valentini*), a Moorish Idol, some dark brown hemirhamphids (halfbeaks) with long beaks and short bodies.

We sailed half an hour late because we had so many officials on board from the immigration authorities and the like who would not leave the ship. There was a moment of drama when it was disclosed that a passenger had changed a $100 note and been given rupiahs for $1,000. This was the Italian countess ('Lady Godiva without horse') who did not know this had happened and did not understand Lyall Watson's first announcement of the circumstances! However all was straightened out.

I saw one Brahminy Kite circling over the town when we were ashore.

Chaetodon punctato-fasciatus
Eniwetok
Maug, Marianas
Saipan

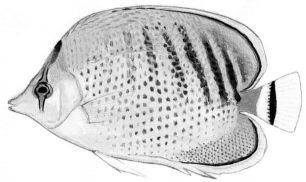

Helen Reef, Carolines
Obi Latu

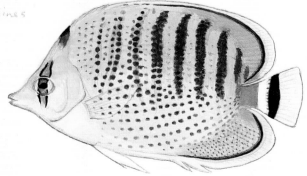

C. pelewensis

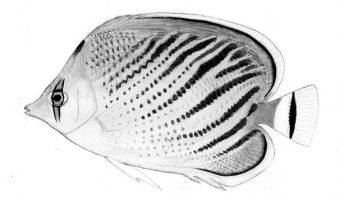

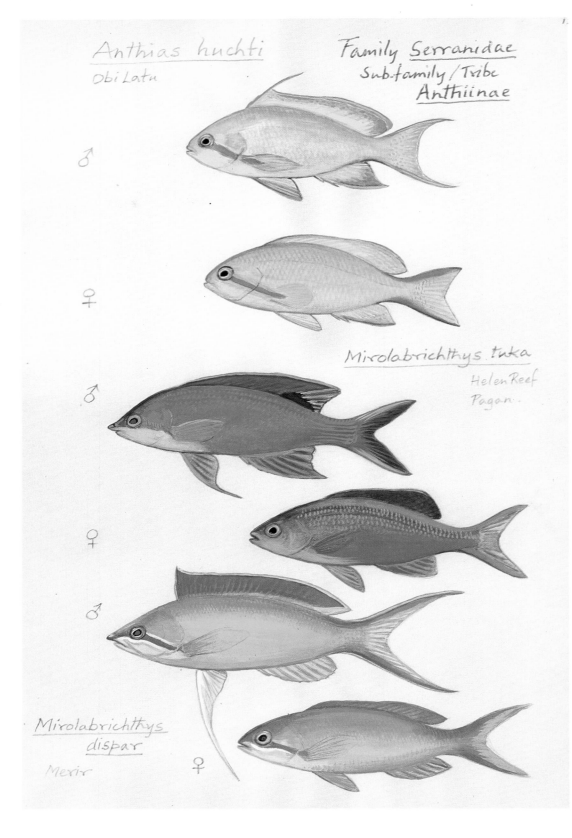

Anthias huchti
Obi Latu

Family Serranidae
Sub-family / Tribe
Anthiinae

♂

♀

Mirolabrichthys tuka
HelenReef
Pagan.

♂

♀

♂

Mirolabrichthys
dispar

Merir

♀

MONDAY 23 AUGUST

Tjiku-hai village on the island of Obi Latu in the Moluccas. A delightful village at the head of a bay where all was picturesque and delightful. Two short swims on the reefs on either side of the bay. Water a little murky but plenty of fish. An hour ashore in the village. Lots of interesting birds in the trees around the village, especially near a bridge leading to the Head Man's house and the school, a delightful house standing by itself. John Stubenbord [the ship's doctor] held a clinic in the Head Man's house.

Then out to the reef at about 1015. First goggling then bubbling till just after 1200. Went down to 60 feet with Valerie [Taylor] and Soames [Summerhays]. Rather dark and murky, but some good fishes down there including *Genicanthus lamark* and *Centropyge bicolor*.

In the afternoon we saw sperm whales.

Amblyglyphidodon aureus

Pterocaesio pisang? pink

Caesio – golden stripe

TUESDAY 24 AUGUST

Mbuang-mbuang on Little Salue Island – one of the Banggai Archipelago. First ashore to one of the most attractive villages we have been to. Houses on stilts along the beach. The whole village was spotlessly clean. Most of the inhabitants were away working at the crops which they went to by canoe across a lagoon which lay behind the hill at the back of the village street. It was a totally unexpected visit and the welcome was very friendly from those few who were there.

After an hour we took two zodiacs across the bay to the edge of a reef, seeing brown Spinner Dolphins (perhaps 100 in the school) but they had passed us, so there was no chance to get into the water with them. In their spinning leaps they must achieve at least two revolutions of the body. It is an amazing thing to see.

Pterocaesio tile

Lutjanus biguttatus

Val, Soames and I had bottles, the rest were snorkelling. I saw 5 sharks of 3 species. Three were fairly large – 6 to 7 feet long. They did not trouble us, but were moving quite fast at times.

Wonderful Jewel Fish (*Anthias*), 2 species of *Anampses* wrasse, also *Pseudodax* wrasse. 15 butterfly fish (between Phil and me) – including 2 we have not yet seen this time: *Coradion altivelis* and *Chaetodon bennetti*. The Sapphire Surgeon Fish (*Paracanthurus hepatus*) was there, and a black and white fish I could not identify at all.

Eupomacentrus sp.? apicalis

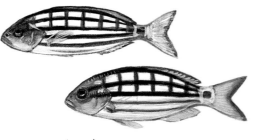

Lutjanus decussatus

Pseudocheilinus octotaenia

Pseudochromis
porphyreus

Naso hexacanthus

Chromis retrofasciatus

Mirolabrichthys
tuka ♂

Mirolabrichthys
tuka ♀

???

Juv.
Bodianus anthioides

WEDNESDAY 25 AUGUST

Buton Island. On the way through the straits we saw thousands of very large fruit bats in the trees. We landed at 0800 on the jetty at Baubau among huge crowds of welcoming Indonesians, '*Salamat pagi*', with 200 handshakes along a corridor of Buton Islanders dressed in their best, many with golden dollars as the centrepiece of an elaborate necklace. The atmosphere was warmly welcoming and the people were charming. It was the beginning of a wonderful day.

First there was a reception with a dance of welcome at the Governor's Residence. He is virtually dictator of the island and

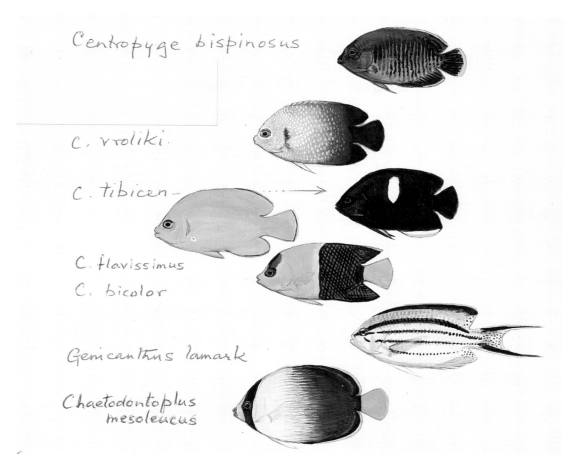

Centropyge bispinosus

C. vroliki.

C. tibicen

C. flavissimus
C. bicolor

Gemicanthus lamark

Chaetodontoplus
mesoleucus

son of the old King (Sultan and Chief). Then, in a convoy of small vans, we travelled through the town, over a suspension bridge by the fish market and up the hill to an old fort, built against invasions from Ternate in the north and Java to the south.

From the fort we went further up the hill among crowds of people to the Sultan's Palace where a huge feast had been prepared – it being the eve of Ramadan. All this had been prearranged by Lorne Blair (who had been at Beaudesert School near Slimbridge where he had a white-backed Carrion Crow chick which I was asked to look at in the long ago).

Lorne is now Indonesianized, having made two films about them (produced by Ringo Starr). He speaks the language fluently, and has a preoccupation with blood. His company is called Cut Throat Productions. But he is a very good talker and an engaging personality – and very knowledgeable about Indonesian history.

The feast was immensely colourful, the food was interesting and sometimes delicious, the dancing of a high standard and the singing charming, though with what seemed to me to be some missionary hymn overtones.

It was rather hot, but absolutely enjoyable.

Opposite: Dancers at Baubau on Buton Island

Grey-headed
Fishing Eagle
Icthyophaga
ichthyaetus

THURSDAY 26 AUGUST

Komodo Island. A pair of Grey-headed Fishing Eagles, *Icthyophaga icthyaetus*, and their flying eaglet were soaring round, and sometimes landing on the headland.

The object of this day was to show to the *Lindblad Explorer*'s passengers the great monitor lizards, known as Komodo Dragons. They grow to more than 10 feet long and can swallow the head of a goat, horns and all. They are, therefore, potentially quite dangerous to humans.

We have visited Komodo six times now and on the first occasion, and one subsequent one, we went ashore to see the dragons. On our earliest visit there were two places this could be done. One was a short walk of about a mile to a dried-up, sandy riverbed where there was a 15-foot high cliff on the outside of one of the river bends. At this point a dead goat would be hung, out of reach of the dragons, on a tree overhanging the riverbed a day or two before our arrival. When the party had assembled a few yards back from the cliff-edge, the goat would be cut down and, when the dragons had started feeding, the on-lookers would creep up, look over the edge and take photographs. This site was known as the 'Short Walk'.

There was also the 'Long Walk' (about four hours out and back) which led to a spot, over a steepish mountain and down the other side, where there was a similar arrangement with a dead goat in a tree. I only went on the 'Short Walk' but Philippa went on the 'Long Walk' twice, and more recently on the 'Short Walk'. On one of her 'Long Walks' she was able to touch one of the great animals when it was sated with goat meat.

The story is told that on one occasion a party on the 'Long Walk' found there were no dragons waiting under the goat, in fact no dragons in sight. They climbed sadly back to the top of the ridge, but having reached it, looked back and saw that the dragons had arrived. They decided to go down again to get their photographs, except for one elderly member of the party who had done enough climbing for one day. He said that he would wait for them on the ridge.

When, in due course, they returned he was nowhere to be seen so they presumed he had walked on ahead back to the ship – two hours away. When they got there they found he had not arrived. All that was ever found were his spectacles and binoculars at the crest of the ridge the next day. Whether he had gone to sleep or had a heart attack and been eaten subsequently by the lizards will never be known. It appears that this is not the only instance of the Komodo Dragons eating people.

On more recent visits to Komodo, we have felt that the time is better spent on the marvellous reef in a bay that we found about three miles from the 'dragon' landing place. The snorkelling

Varanus
komodoensis

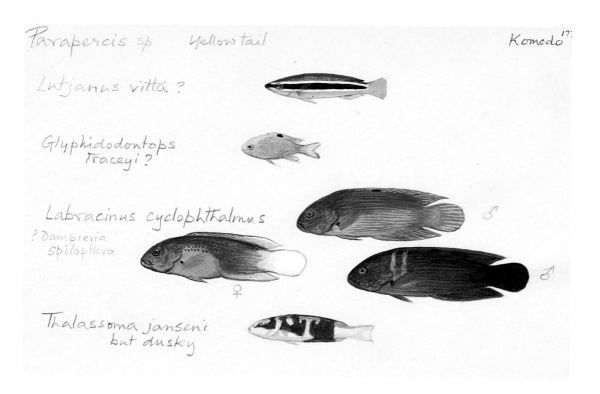

Parapercis sp   Yellow tail

Lutjanus vitta ?

Glyphidodontops
    Traceyi ?

Labracinus cyclophthalmus
? Dambieria
    spiloptera

Thalassoma jansenii
    but dusky

lived up to our recollections and included many species that were new to us. My list for 26 August had 74 fish species on it.

FRIDAY 27 AUGUST

Docked in Benoa Harbour, Bali after feverish completion of a list of the fish we have seen on this trip – which passengers like to have. Phil was not too well in the morning, but in spite of feeling poorly she heroically did all the packing. And so to the Bali Beach Hotel – room 1810 – a quarter mile walk from the lobby.

That evening we saw the Ramayanah 'Ballet'; the dancing was absolutely fantastic.

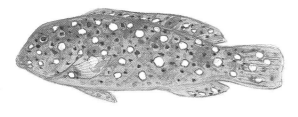

Cirrhitus pinnulatus

Many photographers blocked our view and we decided to move our chairs to block their passage. There were lots of other ways through the tables, and we had moved up so as to be closer. An angry young American photographer took exception. 'You're blocking my way,' said he and pushed past my chair, 'And you're blocking our view,' I replied. Before he returned I closed my chair up to the next, and when he came back there was no passage, although by going to one side of the table he could quite easily have by-passed us. Instead he angrily demanded that I should move out of his way, and when I didn't he hit me, knocking off my specs. Then, I think a little appalled at what he had done, he turned and went round the table. It rather spoiled the middle part of the Ramayanah for me. The chap at the next table, an American, said afterwards that he was about to join in on my side!

SATURDAY 28 AUGUST

In the afternoon Phil and I walked out at low tide across the reef in front of the hotel and tried to launch ourselves for some snorkelling, but it was tricky. There were waves, and when we got through them it was murky as hell. We saw *Acanthurus lineatus*, *Chaetodon vagabundus* and *C. trifascialis*, and a parrot fish. But we decided to turn back. It was altogether too murky. In the shallows on the sill we had seen a 2-foot snake eel which I inadvertently trod on; but it did not seem to be damaged and swam off strongly when I moved my foot.

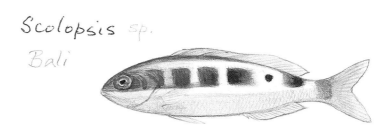

In the evening I began to feel poorly and had a temperature of 100.8°. The coral cut which I got on my ankle about a week ago was painful and inflamed. We got the hotel doctor (Indonesian) with an Indonesian nurse (to translate) to prescribe some antibiotics and a tube of jelly for the infected cut. At bedtime I did not feel very well at all.

SUNDAY 29 AUGUST

I was still not feeling entirely fit but survived a bus day from 0830–1600 which included a visit to the exquisite house of a Dutch painter – Hans Snel – who has a Balinese wife who was a dancer. He is an

Rice paddies, Bali

interesting painter and I liked some of the pictures in his gallery –
portraits and groups including one large abstract. It was fairly
dreadful descending on him in a group. Dr Otto Meissner, who
knew him, and has been on our cruise, introduced us. Meissner
knows Bali well having been here for 5 months 15 years ago. He
mixes trophy hunting with anthropology. He says there never were
any tigers in Bali – only a large jungle cat with spots which is called
a tiger.

The man-made landscapes of Bali are extremely beautiful – the
terraced rice fields, the palms, the great banyan trees and the impeccable taste of the architecture, every house with its temple,
richly ornamented with stone carving. The mosses and liverworts
cover the red brick to give it a wonderful softness.

At the 'Elephant Caves' there were quite a number of birds in

39

At the Elephant Caves there were quite a number of birds in the red blossom-laden upper branches of a great tree, including a male Red-throated Barbet, which went

Megalamia mystacophanes
Red-throated Barbet

several times into a hole, woodpecker-like, on the underside of a dead branch where presumably it had young. Other birds there were a dark blue glossy Flowerpecker, & a whiteye. We also went down among the terraced rice paddies along the great flight of steps which we visited 3 years ago. I did not feel well enough to go to the Kecek Dance, but Phil went and enjoyed it very much. I joined the group for dinner after.

the red blossom-laden upper branches of a great tree, including a male Red-throated Barbet, which went several times into a hole, woodpecker-like, on the underside of a dead branch where presumably it had young. Other birds there were a dark blue glossy flowerpecker, and a white-eye.

And so home a couple of days later.

40

CHAPTER 2

China and Mongolia

DIARY 32   1978

Philippa and I first visited China and Mongolia in the summer of 1978. We were to be the naturalists for a Lindblad land tour of 24 people, some of whom we already knew from the *Lindblad Explorer*. We set off from England for another long absence only 16 days after we had returned, with our daughter Dafila, from the expedition to Arctic Siberia, (described in *Travel Diaries of a Naturalist II*). This was to be a monumental journey beginning with China and Mongolia, continuing to Tokyo, then Hong Kong to join 'the little red ship' – *Lindblad Explorer* – through the Philippine Islands to Sandakan in Sabah, and thence west to Moscow, to enter the USSR, and a third of the way back again to Ashkhabad in Turkmeniya for the General Assembly of the International Union for Conservation of Nature and Natural Resources.

SUNDAY 6 AUGUST 1978

Departure at 0930 from Slimbridge was more than usually 'last-minute-ish'. We have had rather a desperate time since we got back from Siberia with the aftermath of that trip and preparations for this one.

Dafila and Falcon were at home and at about 0600 they began to move around and by 0700 they'd gone. I decided to start *my* day at six because I had three letters to write to Prince Philip, parts of which I had drafted last night. One was about launching the Wild-fowl Trust Appeal next spring, the second was about Prince Philip's visit to Oman early next year and the third was a brief report on our last expedition. A fourth letter had to be written to Prince Charles inviting him to be President of the Wildfowl Trust which I fear he is unlikely to accept [in the event he did and is now the President]. We were due to leave at 0930 and the last letter was finished at 0935. I dictated letters all the way to the airport as I drove.

Although we were at Heathrow an hour and ten minutes before flight time, and it was a 747 jumbo, there were no seats in the non-smoking areas and we couldn't even get seats next to each other – only across the aisle. *Not* an auspicious start for our flight to Hong Kong stopping at Rome, Bahrain and Bangkok. After Bangkok Phil and I were able to sit together for our final lunch in the plane before arrival in Hong Kong. I have had less than half an hour's sleep since 0600 on Sunday and it's now 0830 Monday by my watch which still shows British Summer Time.

MONDAY 7 AUGUST

Arrived Hong Kong. Our 26th wedding anniversary. A taxi through the tunnel to the island and the Hilton Hotel. Edith Macausland, who is 'Hostess' or 'Group Leader' of our party came to our room. She is charming and promises to be most efficient.

We drank vodka and ate nuts in our room before going to bed. After 21 hours flying we were good for little else.

Phil is worse affected by time changes than I. She was awake for an hour in the night but I managed to collect almost 10 hours of sleep and felt much better on . . . .

TUESDAY 8 AUGUST

Baggage outside the door at 0630 to be in the lobby having break-fasted at 0730, there to meet the other people going with us.

So we set off from the Hong Kong Hilton for China – first stop Kwangchow (one time Canton). Hong Kong station is quite fine and the train left according to schedule at 0818 (spot on). We were in the air-conditioned part of the First Class at the front of the train. The journey to the border at Shumchum took about an hour stopping at several stations on the way. We passed some quite nice scenery along the coast although the mess at some of the river mouths had to be seen to be believed. Finally the train stopped, we climbed down and cleared Hong Kong formalities in a crowded building and walked across a bridge over a small river. The bridge had a roof over it, semicircular in section. This is the famous bridge 'to China', and I walked over trailing my little trolley with some of our hand baggage on it. Once across we were in more spacious buildings – at one time climbing two long flights of stairs to the customs clearance. The uniformed officials of the People's Republic were charming, smiling and efficient. In between one process and another we sat in large waiting rooms with armchairs covered in white loose covers. Eventually we came downstairs and boarded the train that would take us on the 2-hour journey to Kwangchow (known also as Guangzhou).

The coach was large as befits a train that doesn't have to bother with tunnels, and the seats were in pairs and revolving – for when the train goes the other way. The back of each seat carried large double metal foot rests. It was very hot and a lady plied us with tea. She first gave each of us a large china mug with a lid and some dry jasmine tea in the bottom, then she brought a huge kettle and poured the hot water into each mug, later topping it up with more water several times. (When we reached our destination she was down on the platform and shook hands with each of us as we descended.)

We rode through small wooded hills and there were rice paddies in the valleys; occasionally there was terracing up the slopes, reminiscent of Bali. Many of the villages had square towers dating from much earlier times. The roofs of the houses were tiled indicating they have heavy rainfall. It was a day of broken cloud which looked as though it would build to rain and did.

Gradually the country grew flatter and we were clearly in the flood plain of a large river with high barren banks. We crossed several waterways with brown muddy waters. Maybe these were all part of the delta of the Pearl River on which Kwangchow is situated.

Besides rice fields there were many other crops – sugar cane, tapioca, beans growing up sticks, and patches of a tall plant (7–8 feet) which may have been Jerusalem artichokes.

Only in one place did we see a group of birds. These were Cattle Egrets (we had seen larger flocks in the New Territories before crossing the border). The only other birds were occasional single unidentified small brown ones – possibly Tree Sparrows. There were flocks of tame ducks and lots of domestic Water Buffalo. In the villages were tame chickens and once we saw some geese.

The architecture of the villages was undistinguished although it had a certain homogeneity. It did not look 'Chinese'. The people looked cheerful whenever we could see them close enough. The trees were interesting. All along the railway line were *Eucalyptus* and *Casuarina*.

On arrival in Kwangchow we emerged into a huge crowd outside the station. Had they come to look at the tourists? A militiaman had to clear a way through the crowd for us to get to our bus – led there by our white-coated girl guide.

The hotel – called the Tungfang Hotel – is quite close to the station. It is a huge 11-storey building in a square pattern with a nicely laid out garden in the middle. Our room – 1981 on the 9th floor – has its own bathroom in the standard hotel pattern. We had lunch – a typical Chinese meal and very good – before going to our rooms.

At 1530 we set off by bus to see the town. They took us first to the Chenhai (or Zhen Hai) Tower – an impressive five storey red building of ancient traditional style. We climbed to the 5th floor for a view over the city. The building is a museum. The view unimpressive. The most striking thing about it to me was the incredible amount of smoke pollution. No clean air programme operating here!

White-breasted Kingfisher.

After that we toured the city and went down to the waterfront along the Pearl River. It was 'rush hour' and the streets were full of bicyclists and pedestrians. Some of the older narrower streets were picturesque but the bulk of the building is uninspiring.

So back to the Tungfang Hotel and another Chinese meal at the end of our first day in China. Very hot night with fan going – temperature barely came below 90°. Phil still troubled by time change.

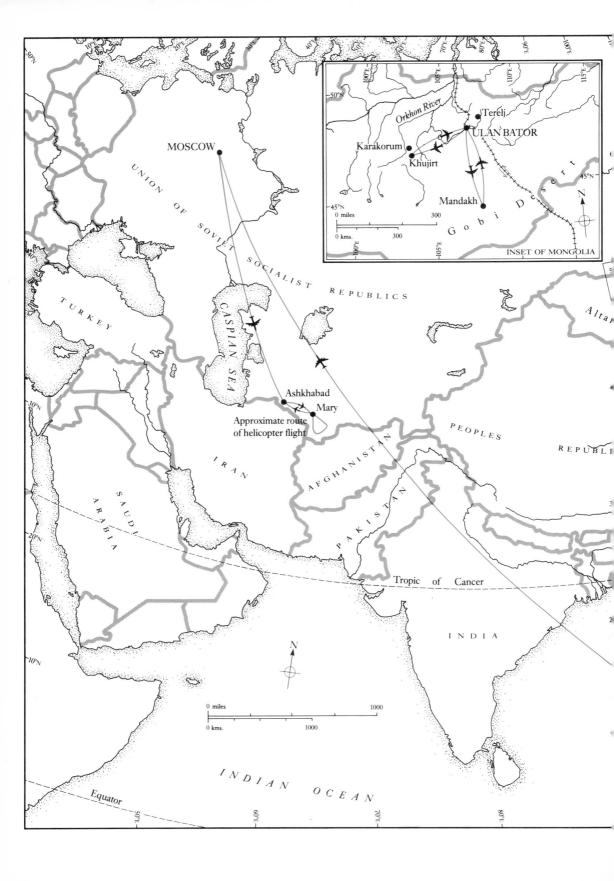

MOSCOW

UNION OF SOVIET SOCIALIST REPUBLICS

TURKEY

CASPIAN SEA

Ashkhabad

Mary

Approximate route
of helicopter flight

IRAN

AFGHANISTAN

PAKISTAN

PEOPLES

REPUBLI

Altai

SAUDI
ARABIA

Tropic   of   Cancer

INDIA

N

10°N

0 miles   1000

0 kms.   1000

INDIAN   OCEAN

Equator

INSET OF MONGOLIA

Orkhon River

Tereli

ULAN BATOR

Karakorum

Khujirt

Mandakh

Gobi Desert

45°N

0 miles   300

0 kms.   300

N

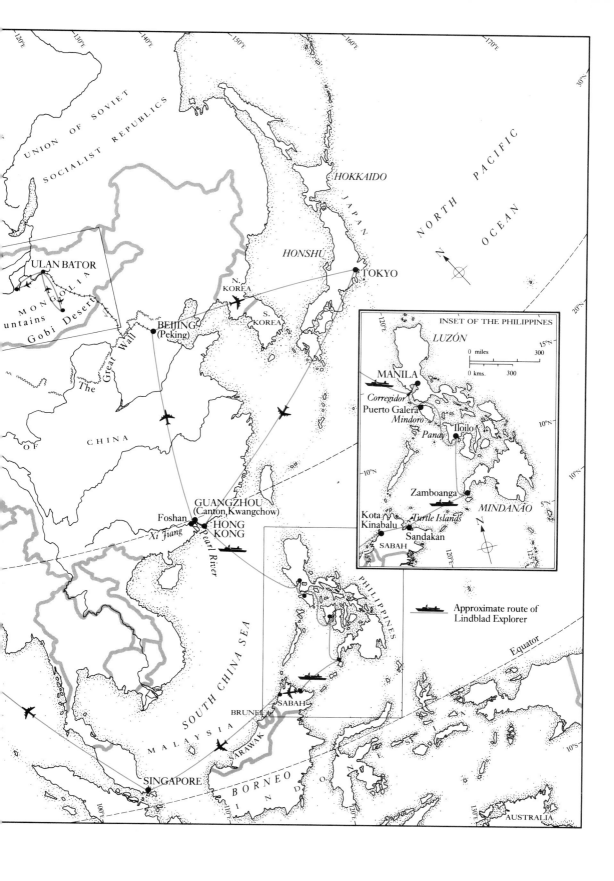

Barge and landing stage on Pearl River, Kwangchow

WEDNESDAY 9 AUGUST

I tried Chinese breakfast: savoury rice gruel with liver, cold egg and meatball fritter but I didn't risk a strange translucent object looking vaguely like a shell-denuded mollusc. Also a white roll, a doughnut type bun and a sweet cake. I think the Western breakfast – also on offer – might have suited me better.

Our bus took us to a small river steamer and for 2½ hours we steamed first down the river and back, then up stream and back. We enjoyed it very much, mainly because of the vast variety of boats and methods of propulsion – though only one sailing junk. We sat four to a table with a Belgian couple from a different tour, and next to some Dutch. There was a good deal of high cloud about and the scene was for the most part in monochrome – no bright colours, only shades of brown on the turbid brown water. There were barges loaded with sand or mud with their families living in the high stern, the scullers – sometimes two to a great oar moving in supple unison, sometimes balancing far out on a transverse plank – the occasional old houses with picturesque roofs, and the ugly multi-storey dwelling houses brought to life by the washing out to dry from nearly every window. A kaleidoscope of vivid impressions of a functional but rather cheerful society. The population of this rather small city is over 2 million and smiling and laughing faces

46

seem widespread. Only one bird seen on this trip – a Tree Sparrow under one of the bridges.

Back for lunch to our huge hotel. The dining rooms are air-conditioned. We eat in one of two neighbouring rooms each of

Passer montanus.
Tree Sparrow
The urban sparrow of the Far East.

Carduelis sinica
Chinese Greenfinch.

which has space for 400 people sitting round tables for 8. Being 24 our group has 3 tables. At some meals both rooms are virtually full – all tourists. There are a number of other dining rooms on various floors in the huge building so we think that no less than 1,000 people are staying and eating in the hotel. The Chinese food is very good, very varied, full of garlic for the most part and, with the exception of the rice, not very fattening. Green ginger is a fairly frequent ingredient which I like and Phil doesn't. To drink there is a fizzy orange, a fizzy clear lemonade, some pretty nasty beer without any potency whatever, and mineral water.

After lunch we were taken first to an ivory-carving factory. It was fascinating to see the 'mass production' techniques mixed up with the art and skill of the individual carver. To begin with they sat us round a table loaded with large, ornate and, for the most part, rather ugly but hugely elaborate examples of the art. We were told that an ivory ball consisting of concentric independent spheres free to revolve inside each other would take a carver a year to complete, and some of the designs would take three times that long.

At the end of the preliminary lecture there were a good many questions, some of which touched on the survival of the elephants. Where did the ivory come from? 'Overseas.' Where did the carvings sell? 'Eighty per cent for export.' My question: What would happen to the factory if there were no more elephants? was answered with 'We would carve in jade or wood – it wouldn't matter'. 'Ivory is much more expensive to buy than it used to be', came in answer to another question.

Azure-winged Magpie
Cyanopica cyana

It was rather sad to be so ambivalent about the carvers' art. Conservation demands disapproval but the aesthetic appeal of some of the work was moving, especially watching the work take shape. I watched one girl graving out the tail of a bird. She had no drawing to refer to – although some of them had. We saw one chap working on a boat and were told it was a 3-year project.

While we were there there was a power cut – not however a strike by the Electrical Workers' Union, but a failure of their own factory generator and after five minutes it was repaired. As we were leaving there was some confusion over who could buy ivory and some were learning, for the first time, that it could not be legally brought into the United States.

The afternoon was rainy, for it is the monsoon season, but in spite of that we went to the Zoo. The ostensible reason was for the group to see the Giant Pandas. The Zoo is free and very spacious but not really very good.

THURSDAY 10 AUGUST
Out of Kwangchow by a very busy road in our bus, across two arms of the Pearl River into the rice paddies, and thence 10 miles to the city of Foshan which once had a population estimated at 2 million and now has only $\frac{1}{4}$ million. Even 10 years ago it was said to be 350,000. It was a centre of ironworks, but is now said to be most famous for its pottery, in a suburb 6 kilometres out called Shihwan – but it was a disappointing place. We saw all kinds of statuettes – people, buffalos, lions, birds – being prepared for the kilns. Virtually all of the work they were mass producing was without any artistic merit. It was almost totally representational and there did not seem to be the vestige of an original sculptural idea to be seen. To see all these people labouring to reproduce such poor original work was deeply depressing.

Red-rumped Swallow.

Back in Foshan the 'Ancestral Temple', now of course a museum, was quite different. It was full of beautiful things – roofs, sculpture, pictures, temple furniture, etc. A most wonderful place with some nice butterflies in the gardens. Quite lovely. Huge *papier mâché* guilded figures towered menacingly, leaning over you in rows as you went in – with one finger of the left hand raised in admonition and the right hand armed with sword or hammer to strike.

After the Ancestral Temple came lunch in the Overseas Chinese Hotel – a rather simpler meal than in the Tungfang in Kwangchow, with less gravy and no garlic in any of the dishes.

Across the road was the student Arts Centre where they were making lanterns, prints, cut-outs and drawings. Here was original work – some quite interesting. There was a big wash drawing of horses with a lot of action (for sale at £35) which I liked but others thought the Chinese characters the only artistic things in the room.

On the way back from Foshan we saw (?) migrating Red-rumped Swallows and stopped near a farm among the rice paddies for

49

photography. We walked down a lane and were greeted with grins and giggles by 30 or 40 farm workers. We asked if Phil could take photographs and it was agreed, but many hid themselves – in doorways, half behind bushes or just by turning away. There were beautifully shaped pottery jars full of fertilizer, and water buffalos.

Back in Kwangchow we spent half an hour in the park which is devoted to the memory of the Martyrs of the Kwangchow Uprising in 1927 (when 5,000 were killed) who are apparently buried under a large mound on a hill. In the *Casuarina* trees beside the mound I heard and saw Chinese Greenfinches and white-eyes, the latter *very* noisy. They seemed to have grown young and I saw what was probably their best nest in the upper branches. There was a lake with boats on it – which some of our party tried out. Bridges and pagodas round and in the lake were attractively designed. I was having some tummy trouble and only just got back to the hotel in time! We decided not to go out to the restaurant for dinner.

FRIDAY 11 AUGUST
A good long night to catch up on the remains of our jet-lag. But in the morning Phil was doubled up with tummy pains. So I sat with my darling all morning and she slept a little. After lunch I brought her up some lychees. She was much better.

By 1520 we were off in the bus to the airport. A very new TU 132 jet (equivalent to a Boeing 707) took us to Peking (Beijing), avoiding

Buffalo and farm hand near Kwangchow on the way back from Foshan

Fictitious animal in the
avenue leading to the Ming
Tombs

the biggest thunder clouds, in $2\frac{1}{2}$ hours with a cold snack meal. To
the disappointment of some we are not staying in the Peking Hotel
but in a small olde worlde one called the Nationalities Hotel=
Minzu Fandian.

SATURDAY 12 AUGUST
Morning in the Forbidden City – the Imperial Palace – mainly built
in the Ming Dynasty (1368–1644) but lived in by Emperors thereafter. It was a hot morning and the place was crowded – about 80%
being local people. Without question the buildings are superlatively
beautiful; rather surprisingly water areas are almost totally absent,
except for the moat itself, so reflections of elegant architecture have
not been contrived. But the harmony of style, the beauty of the

51

colours – the golden yellow glaze of the roof tiles, the blue and red and gold of the friezes, the dark red of the walls and the green of the occasional trees (Pines, False Cypress, Pomegranate etc.) produced an overwhelming impression of artistry and 'good taste'. Every prospect seemed to please. It was a fantastic feast for the eye.

Curious features: an old lady with bound feet, absolutely minute – six inches long – having difficulty walking on them, the overwhelming smell of garlic in the jewel rooms and other crowded places, the loud singing of the cicadas, the number of soldiers (on holiday) in the crowd and three sailors in blue uniforms.

The birds seen were Jungle Crow, Swift and Tree Sparrow, and there were great quantities of a large *Aeshna* dragonfly.

In the afternoon we were fetched by the Chief of the Commercial/ Economic Section of the US Liaison Office, Bill Thomas, to go to the zoo. We saw five Giant Pandas in the indoor cages. There were two young ones in a terribly small cage obviously bored to tears and moving in a pattern which included a kind of somersault. Pathetic. The four Lesser Pandas looked happier in their outdoor den, but were obviously much too hot – high 80°s.

The waterfowl enclosure had walled sides and smallish islands but a remarkable collection of waterbirds and cranes. The most exciting things were a merganser drake in eclipse which I believe might have been a Chinese Merganser (the scapulars – white with black edges, and the well marked flanks did not seem right for the Red-breasted Merganser)* and the Black-necked Cranes from Tibet which are short-necked and rather small – the body off-white or very pale buffish grey.

The crane collection was striking – nine kinds. There was one young crane – possibly *japonensis* [Japanese Crane]. A terrible covered 'chicken run' held a pair of Siberian White Cranes which looked in very good condition. The accommodation was appalling – a peninsula in the lake covered with *ad hoc* chicken runs netted over the top. However I got the feeling that the husbandry might not be too bad.

The Chilean Flamingos had 3 young with them, and a fourth one was apparently being hand-raised. A pair of Mute Swans had nested successfully and the near fully-grown cygnets were in another 'chicken run'. Another lake was full of Whooper Swans – perhaps fifty – with eight Bewick's.

SUNDAY 13 AUGUST

At 0800 our bus drew into the huge main square of Peking – 98 acres in extent. At one end of the square is the Mao Tse Tung Mausoleum, at the other the entrance to the Forbidden City, in the middle a kind of Cenotaph to the Heroes of the People's Republic, and at one side the Great Hall of the People. Presently we were formed up

* Afterwards I established that it was *not* a Chinese Merganser.

into a queue 'in columns of fours' and fed in at the side of a much longer queue of Chinese people waiting in orderly lines. Mao's body is kept in refrigeration and is only on view three days a week. We were warned that there must be no cameras with us and we should conduct ourselves with due reverence.

When we were inside the huge building the column was split down the middle – two going left – two sharp right past a huge land-scape painting. Then the columns came back towards each other to pass on either side of the bier. Mao was easily recognizable – the famous wart on his chin standing out, his temples wrinkled. The Chinese passing on the other side stopped to bow which did not seem incumbent on us. We walked slowly past, and out of the chamber before rejoining the right hand column and finally passing out of doors on the opposite side of the building.

A quick visit to the zoo and cool enough for the pandas to be out of doors. They were shut in again while we were there. Then to the Summer Palace with 20,000 Chinese.

MONDAY 14 AUGUST

The Great Wall. To think of it running for 6,000 kilometres is mind-boggling. It goes to the top of every hill so that every reconnaissance point is occupied and defended by a fort. The traditional concept is of a scaly dragon winding endlessly over the hills – it would still block the way of an army with tanks.

The only birds we saw were swallows. There were no humans

53

or human habitations in sight among the hills so one wonders 'why so few birds?' Time of year, heat of the day, they've eaten them all, or killed them with pesticides? But 6 kinds of butterflies, cicadas singing everywhere, and grasshoppers. Maybe just time of year and time of day.

Back into the train and a box lunch on the way down the mountain. At a station out in the plain we got out and found our bus waiting to take us to the Ming Tombs – 13 of them are in the valley, but only one has been excavated. Huge vaults deep in the ground containing some great boxes (which apparently are replicas of those found there with the imperial skeletons and treasure) defended by huge marble doors. The treasure – including two very fine lapis lazuli crowns and much gold plate – was housed in a pavilion above ground.

The nicest thing at the Ming Tombs was the avenue of stone animals – lions, camels, elephants, one of the nine sons of the dragon, and horses. It was an hour and a half bus ride back to Peking through fields of maize, kaffir corn, sorghum, sesame, aubergines, cotton, etc.

TUESDAY 15 AUGUST

The Day of the Banquets. As instructed we waited in our room for a phone call from an interpreter who would take us to the meeting with Mr Qu Geping and Dr Zheng Zhoxin. The call would come between 0930 and 0945 for a 1000 meeting. At 1010 a feverish call: could we come at once in a taxi to the Peking Hotel? We did so, but no one was there to meet us. It transpired that I had never told the Embassy that Phil was with me, so they were not looking for a couple. Eventually the girl interpreter found us and we were ushered in to see Mr Qu (pronounced Chu) who is Permanent Representative at UNEP [United Nations Environment Programme] and head of the Environmental Protection Office of the State Council in China.

Later Dr Zheng (pronounced Cheng) arrived in a blue grey Chinese suit. He was entirely delightful with a splendid twinkle in his eye and a lively sense of humour. He had just received the Red Data Book [on endangered species]. *Galliformes* [game birds] are out for China and *Anseriformes* [ducks, swans and geese] will come next. He is China's foremost ornithologist.

Dr Zheng gave me a poster of China's endangered species – which included a few problematical ones. For instance when I pointed to the Great One Horned Rhino and said, 'How many of these in China?' he replied promptly, 'None, but they might walk over into Tibet'. When I asked him about *Grus japonensis* [Japanese Crane] numbers he said there were 300–400 birds breeding in north eastern China near Qiqihaer in a marsh surrounded by rivers. I asked if the marsh was liable to be drained and he said, 'Not for the present, but of course you cannot be certain about the future'. Then he said, 'Your visit will be a good stimulus', after which he proceeded to explain to

Male golden lion in the Forbidden City

Mr Qu what we had been talking about. He didn't think the Crested Shelduck could be surviving. The Eastern White Stork – which he had no reason to suppose was more than a subspecies of *C. ciconia* [Western White Stork]* – was certainly only to be seen in a few hundreds. I told him they were extinct in Japan. He thought the lack of trees in China might be one of the causes. When I asked about *Mergus squamatus* [Chinese Merganser] he said that the first nest had recently been found, to everyone's surprise, in a hole in a *tree*! It was on the slope of the Everwhite Mountain (Changbai Shan) which lies on the border of China with North Korea.

We greatly liked Dr Zheng whose ambition it is to come to Slimbridge. We hope he achieves it. [He did in 1979.]

* I am convinced that the Eastern White Stork is specifically distinct and should be *C. boyciana*, not *C. c. boyciana*.

At the end of the meeting Mr Qu announced that we would move into the next room for a banquet. We said alas we did not know this had been arranged and were already committed to a different banquet in the same hotel. From the expression on their faces it was clear that we were about to give terrible offence if we did not accept their invitation, so we moved into the next room and sat down. We had to try to judge how much we needed to eat for honour to be satisfied and at the end of the first course, which was a meal in itself, we took our leave as graciously as we could. We then shot off and found the private room booked by the American Hotel Promoter Marshall Coyne who had invited us to his lunch for the Chinese Minister of Culture. We arrived *just* before they sat down. We were introduced also to the head of tourism and a number of Ambassadors, including Philippines, Sri Lanka, etc. The 11 course meal included *bêche de mer*, squid and other goodies and we consumed a great deal of *mao tai*.

In the evening we went with a group to a restaurant called the Peking Duck where we ate Peking duck which was quite good though our hearts were not really in more food after the orgy at lunch time.

WEDNESDAY 16 AUGUST

By train across the mountains to the Gobi Desert of Inner Mongolia. The train kept extremely good time – starting at 0805 and following the same track we had travelled on to the Great Wall on Monday. Our four bunk compartment was shared with Bob and Mimi Abington – he a doctor in general practice and she a discerning gentle person with a strong aesthetic sense. She is diabetic. They were delightful travelling companions.

The day was fine and sunny. To begin there were as few birds as we have become used to expecting in China. Eventually we passed three Black Storks which rose about 150 yards out from the train. After the line turned north we passed through steppes that seemed to be almost totally flat. The grass and other plants were extremely sparse.

The telegraph poles and wires carried a few birds at last: some very small falcons (? Red-footed), some Hoopoes, some wheatears and a large pale buzzard which seems likely to have been *Buteo hemilasius*, the Upland Buzzard. There were some shallow pools on which were Green, Wood and Common Sandpipers, some terns, and an unfamiliar gull which may have been *Larus relictus* [the rare Relict Gull]. There were also some teal and some larger unidentified ducks against the light. A dove was presumably *Streptopelia orientalis* [Rufous Turtle Dove].

At the frontier with Mongolia the railway changes to a wider gauge. We were offered the choice of seeing a film in the local cinema or staying in the sleeper to watch the fascinating process of changing the wheels. We stayed on the train and stood in our pyjamas to watch the operations. The coaches were spaced out and each body jacked up – and we were in our turn – so that the narrow gauge wheels could be rolled out into the space between the coaches. At this point an overhead transporter crane picked them up and put them on a parallel siding and then brought in the replacement wide gauge bogeys. It was all done with amazing speed and efficiency.

THURSDAY 17 AUGUST

The desert steppe of the Gobi. I awoke as the sun was rising. It shone under the train casting its shadow on the slightly undulating steppe and there was a rainbow that was almost all red because of the red sunrise. We had evidently traversed the driest part of the Gobi Desert during darkness. Now it was steppe rather than desert. We had a Mongolian Restaurant Car and the food was substantially more primitive.

Merlin after
Flycatcher.

During breakfast 8 waterfowl flew in a flock parallel to the train, but against the light. Were they Ruddy Shelducks or geese? Their necks were rather short. It was most tantalizing as they finally converged with the train and flew over it and we shall never be sure – though I am virtually certain they were Ruddies. We passed many pairs and small parties of Demoiselle Cranes. Hoopoes were very numerous as were also white-headed buzzards which were either Long-legged or Upland Buzzards – *Buteo rufinus* or *B. hemilasius* – both of which have light and dark phases, as in *B. buteo* [Common Buzzard].

I had two special excitements. First, I saw a large immature falcon

Red-breasted Flycatcher
Ficedula parva
albicilla

Peter Scott.

彼德・斯克特.

Sat. 19.8.78
Coach trip to Terelj. 2½ hours from Ulan Bator ESE. 80
Glorious sunny day with a few cumulus clouds. Rather cool
After crossing the Toal (Tuul) River, a paved road for
35 km then dirt road with much dust across rolling
steppe, up into the mountains & sparse woods.
Most numerous birds — Choughs.
Marvellous wild flowers. Phil's cold much better.

Birds

Raven
Magpie
Black Stork
Wheatear
Jackdaw
Chough
Crow
Martin
Grey Wagtail
Tit
Bunting
Swallow
2 Plumbeous Redstart
Red-throated Flycatcher [Breasted]
Arctic Warbler

Grey Crow.

Butterflies

Painted Lady
Small Tortoiseshell.
Small Copper
Ringlet
Argus.

Marmot burrows.

Back at Hotel by 1810.
Dancing to songs after dinner
with fermented mares milk.

Flowers

Purple Iris
   not flowering.
Edelweiss
Great Knapweed
Knapweed
Thyme
Echinops?
Dwarf Michaelmas Daisy
   Aster.
Sorrel
Wild Rhubarb
10 Yellow Bedstraw
Gentian
   Large
Gentian
   Medium
Gentian
   Small
Lousewort
   Yellowish White
Marsh Lousewort
   Deep red. Large
Arnica / Senecio
Cudweed
Wormwood
Dianthus prasinus
   Pink
20 Scabious Scabiosa
   fischeri
Geranium pratense
Purple Milk Vetch
   Astragalus.
Purple Vetch Trifolium
   lupinaster
Larkspur. Large
25 Larkspur Small.
   Delphinium cheilanthum

Burnet
Veronica
Blue Bell flower
Fireweed
   C. angustifolium
Large White Daisy
30 Yarrow
Q. Anne's Lace
   ? Carum
Cistus
Vaccinium
Birch Betula
   fruticosa
Aspen
Larch Larix sibirica
Larch
Pine
Yellow Poppy
40 Poplar
Willow
Meadowsweet
Ranunculus
Campanula
Myosotis
Garlic Chives
   Allium
   polyr.
Cerastium
Yellow Umbellifer
Potentilla
50 Hawksbit
Dandelion
Bistort
Mint
Cress (Pink)
Armeria
5 ? Erigeron

Gentians

Terelj
19. 8. 78

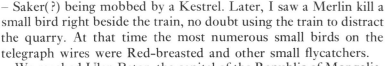

– Saker(?) being mobbed by a Kestrel. Later, I saw a Merlin kill a
small bird right beside the train, no doubt using the train to distract
the quarry. At that time the most numerous small birds on the
telegraph wires were Red-breasted and other small flycatchers.

We reached Ulan Bator, the capital of the Republic of Mongolia,
in the evening.

SUNDAY 20 AUGUST

I have caught Phil's cold and feel lousy!

Lamasery [monastery], Ulan Bator. A marvellous place. Watched
ceremonies in two temples. Drums, cymbals, horns and deep bass
chanting. Barley grains, hot(?) mares' milk. Basic colours red.
Amazing hanging draperies. Pigeon eating grain, quite tame. Many
pigeons outside. Prayer wheels. Old people still needing religion.
Pressing foreheads against relics. All lamas very old except one
young one. Women were officiating. Masses of visual and auditory
impressions. Most exciting.

MONDAY 21 AUGUST

Design on a door
of one of the yurts

Early in the morning we flew by turbo-prop Antonov 24 1½ hours
south west of Ulan Bator to Mandakh in the Gobi Desert. Phil and
I were sitting just behind two locals and the smell of sour milk was
terrible. The plane landed by a village of 36 felt tents or *yurts*

60

Phrynocephalus versicolor. Strauch
Gobi Desert 21.8.78

? sp.

Mon 21 Aug.   Gobi Desert.   Mandokh.

By turbo-prop ~~/~~ from Ulan Bator 1½ hrs
    Antonov 24

1½ hrs bus ride to the Flaming Cliffs — site of Roy Chapman Andrews
   palaeontological dig in 1924.

Hoopoe   Agamid Lizard
Red-throated Flycatcher   ?Agama stolizrana
Yellow Wagtail. Blue headed
Tree Sparrow
Lark. Large reddish   ?Mirafra assamica   Saxaul Trees.
          pale rump.
Short-toed Lark. Calandrella,
                  cheleensis?
Shore Lark
Swallow
Arctic Warbler
10 Black Kite
    Raven

Red-breasted
Flycatcher
Ficedula parva
♀ or immature

    Ruddy Shelduck
    Sand Grouse
    Upland Buzzard
    Pipit ?
    Eagle. ?Booted
    Wheatear
    Desert Wheatear
    Bluethroat
20 Great Grey Shrike
    Saker Falcon
         Falco cherrug.
    Blacktailed Godwit
    Wood Sandpiper
    Mongolian Sand Plover

    Common Gull
26. Finch Lark. Black-faced.
27. Yellow Wagtail ? Black-headed

Hoopoe
Upupa epops

Pallas's Sand Grouse
Syrrhaptes paradoxus

The Flaming Red Cliffs, Gobi Desert

(locally called *gers*), one small stone building, one large *ger* and two open work 'pagodas'. All were fenced into a compound to keep out the camels. This was to be our base for the next two days.

A bus ride to the 'Flaming Cliffs'. The red cliffs where Roy Chapman Andrews made his sensational dinosaur finds in 1924 were spectacular in the afternoon sun, like great red ruins in the surrounding yellow desert. Even the Agamas were red. Maybe this is within the colour change control of the animals or maybe just a local population. It was a long drive with few stops. One was to see some 'Yaks'. These were black and white and may have been descended from Wild Yaks, but they also had a good deal of cattle blood in their veins. On some marshy ground was one very tame Black-tailed Godwit and a Wood Sandpiper as well as the usual assortment of wagtails: Blue-headed, Black-headed *et al* – impossible to distinguish in immature plumage.

We passed and flushed quite a number of sandgrouse which had black bellies – Pallas's? I have yet to get a good view of one.

Beyond the 'Flaming Cliffs' was a forest of Saxaul Trees – the tallest about 12–15 feet high. A pair of Desert Wheatears had a nest in a horizontal rock cleft. Phil saw a Bluethroat – and among the trees was a Great Grey Shrike – with much white on its head.

Tu. 22.8

Bus from Maidoch to the Altai

In camp before leaving: Kestrel
                        Yellow-breasted Bunting

In the Altai:
  Shore lark
  ~~Eagle ? Golden~~
  ~~Serpent Eagle~~
  Green Sandpiper *Tringa ochropus*
  Grey wagtail
  White Wagtail
  Blue headed Wagtail
  Black headed Wagtail
  Grey Wagtail
  Raven
  Rock Pigeon *Columba rupestris*
  Crag Marten
  Kestrel
  Hoopoe
  Wall creeper
  Daurian Redstart
  Mountain Finch →
  ~~Leucosticta~~ ~~nemoricola~~ *Montefringilla*
  Blue Throat
  Lammergeier
  Golden Eagle
     robbing a Buzzard.
  Upland or
  Longlegged Buzzard
  Common Sandpiper
  Richard's Pipit
     or Blyths
  Tawny Pipit
  Red throated Pipit.
  Swift.

Painted Lady
Meadow Brown
? Maniola jurtina
Flightless Grasshopper
   (Tettigonioidea)

and after return
an unidentified Flycatcher (below)

Rock Pigeon
Columba rupestris

Wallcreeper

Lammergeier

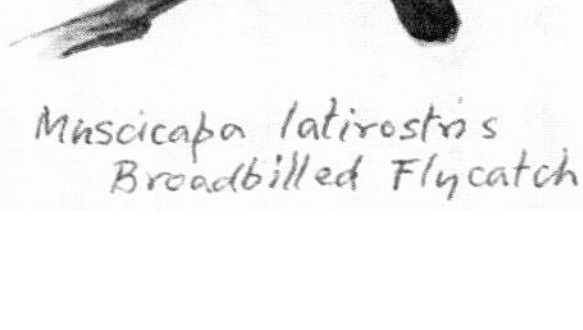

Muscicapa latirostris
Broadbilled Flycatcher

Brown Shrike
Lanius cristatus
Mandoch. Gobi Desert
21. August 1978

Demoiselle Crane
Anthropoides virgo

Gobi Desert
17 - 25 August
1978.

TUESDAY 22 AUGUST

A day in the Altai. A very bumpy drive up the gently sloping steppe into the mountains. I was in the back of the bus with Edie [Edith Macausland] and we spent the time being bounced up and down. We reckoned we must have been weightless for 20% of the time and experiencing 3–4 g for another 20%! It was rugged riding, through rugged country.

From the Calandrella lark country we moved gradually into Wheatear country and then quickly up into rocks and low juniper. At one point we disturbed a group of a dozen Ibex on a hill. At last we reached a picnic site by a small stream. Here was a herd of multi-coloured Yaks with one apparently fairly pure bred bull which had been de-horned.

Upland Buzzard (adult) mobbing Golden Eagle (immature) in the Mongolian Altai. 22.8.78

While the group ran eagerly towards them, whooping with delight, I was preoccupied with a Green Sandpiper and Grey Wagtails. There were lots of birds concentrated along the stream: White Wagtails, some Blue-headed and Black-headed Wagtails. There was a family of Hoopoes moving gently ahead of us.

We made our way along the gorge in the footsteps of a fast-walking Japanese youth. Some of the birds flew high past us and so we re-traced our steps up stream again, coming to a rock wall where two of our party – David Leach and Dick Brush – had been watching a

Peter in the gorge in the Altai Mountains

<u>Wed. 23. Aug.</u>   0630 Bus ride starts for the camels.

Morning flight: Sand Grouse to water in parties of 10-20

Collective
Camel Farm   Mandokh.   Lecture by Khokhoo in the Ger.

640,000 Camels in Mongolia. 200 at this farm.

Used for milk, wool, hide, meat, dung (fuel)

Dung: 1 camel produces 600 pieces of dung per night.
                230 kilos per annum.

They have Camel Races, Camel Carts & Camel Caravans
but we didn't see them.

We drank fermented Camel's milk — yoghurt
and ate camel cheese — very strong
with hard biscuits — very hard.

Winter fodder for Camels includes meals cooked + dried
               (millet, rice, bone meal, horse blood)

               The camels are milked
               2-3 times a day + yield
               1 litre at each milking.

Sand Rat   {   *Meriones meridianus* ? (*meridianalis* ?) Jird.
             or *Rhombomys opimus*, Great Gerbil.
             or *Brachiones przewalskii*. Przewalski's Gerbil.

Lactation period about the same as gestation — 13 months
Camels live 25 – 30 years.

Around the herd of 200 were three ? commensal species
evidently profiting from the camel dung, its insects +
perhaps its effect on the vegetation. These were:
     Wheatear
     Mongolian Sand Plover
     Rodent —

                   Phil + I rode camels,
                   for the sake of pix.

Birds
Sand Grouse
Long-legged Buzzard
Wheatear
Mongolian Sand Plover
Demoiselle Crane 4.
Larks. Short-Toed
        Rufous
        Sky

Wallcreeper. We found it quite quickly and watched it for 20 minutes – it was quite tame, hunting in cracks and crannies within 15 yards of us. There were Crag Martins, kestrels (which may be Lessers – *F. naumanni*) and a flock of 20 plus Rock Pigeons (*C. rupestris*) with a white subterminal band on the tail.

Back in the open area at the mouth of the gorge our picnic lunch of shish kebabs was being prepared with a potential problem involving a lady arranging cucumber slices and salami slices in pretty patterns on the dishes with very dirty fingers!

Bob Abington described a 'Robin-like bird with a red breast'; was this a Rubythroat – or what? I went back down the stream to investigate, and eventually found a cock Daurian Redstart, and a female Bluethroat.

At the picnic site we had a good view of a large pale buzzard with rufous flanks – Long-legged perhaps but more likely to be an Upland. It evidently knew all about picnic sites as sources of food. So too did some finches with white flashes in their wings. Later an immature Golden Eagle came into the valley and made the buzzard give up something in its talons. But the eagle was too shy to go down and collect it. Once I saw a Lammergeier circling high overhead with its oval shaped tail. Altogether a very rewarding bird day.

WEDNESDAY 23 AUGUST

Collective camel farm, Mandakh. 640,000 camels in Mongolia, 200 at this farm. Used for milk, wool, hide, meat, dung (fuel). Around the herd were three commensal species evidently profiting from the camel dung, its insects and perhaps its effect on the vegetation. These were: Wheatear, Mongolian Sand Plover, and Sand Rat.

We drank fermented camel's milk – yoghurt – and ate camel cheese – very strong with hard biscuits – very hard. Phil and I rode camels, for the sake of pictures.

Back at camp there were a few birds around the young irrigated trees along the fence behind the *gers*: a Brown Shrike (*L. cristatus*) had a bath in the pool provided by the leak in the irrigation pipe. Both kinds of flycatchers were there: the one with white in the tail and the one without. The four Demoiselle Cranes were most enjoyable.

At 1130 we took off for Ulan Bator and landed there at 1247. Now we are back in our original room having had an excellent lunch – but only briefly as we set off again for Khujirt tomorrow, no doubt at sparrow fart.

THURSDAY 24 AUGUST

Early start by plane to Khujirt. Grey Crows/Jackdaws with larger crows, choughs [Red-billed] and one Magpie on the way to the airport.

Morning resting. Large late lunch. 1500 departure for a horse farm (220 horses). Demoiselle Cranes on the way. Later a flock of 56 looking marvellous in sunshine with black shower cloud behind.

Yurts at Khujirt horse farm

Juvenile toad at
Khujirt.

After watching the horse farming techniques we repaired to the 'farm buildings' – two *gers* and some heaps of horse manure. So into the largest *ger*. Fermented mares' milk – *airag* – in three wooden barrels. Three kinds of cheese – two mild, one brown and strong – also 'grape nuts'. Stove with big pan of drying cream, fuelled with horse dung. Normal meals are meat with noodles.

Ger very pleasant inside, hung with lace and needlework over the three beds, and frames holding quantities of group photographs, five large wing mirrors, three suitcases set up on painted panels with additional patterns (probably the fronts of chests). The patterned grey felt rugs were made by the family. They move several times a month. It takes one hour to dismantle a *ger*, and the same time to set it up again.

Our *ger* camp at Khujirt is beside the village and next door to a sanatorium set up to make use of a hot spring with a high sulphur content. On the other side of the camp, just beyond our *ger*, is grass steppe rising quickly to rolling hills with some rocky outcrops.

The commonest birds are Tree Sparrows and Black Kites. The latter are apparently *Milvus migrans lineatus*. There are dozens on posts and fences all round our camp in all stages of plumage and moult as many are clearly young of the year. When the sun shines they gather in the small thermals which they do not seem to take to any great height. The other numerous birds are Ravens and choughs and they often fly over the camp calling. The chough calls are quite musical and very pleasant.

70

Chough.

Mongolian Jackdaw.

FRIDAY 25 AUGUST

From Khujirt by bus 2 hours to Karakorum through the South Hangai mountains. It was Genghis Khan's capital and he built it. City completed in 1236, burnt down 1388. Kublai Kahn moved in 1260 to Peking.

As we stood on the mounds where the Palace of Genghis Khan had been excavated – with its stone tortoise and the tomb of the Mother of the First Living God in Mongolia – about 120 Demoiselle Cranes flew towards us, and landed about 200 yards away. They landed in a loose formation with family parties dotted about. Nearest were two families – one with two young and one with one. The male of the larger family showed aggression and the smaller family moved away. I watched them walking quite fast across the hummocky sparse turf, from time to time catching a grasshopper. Beyond them was a much larger flock with not less than 300 birds. These were far out in the flat river plain where the land was mostly under near ripe wheat none of which seemed so far to have been cut. Later these distant cranes were in the air again. I got the impression that some were using the thermals for migration and that we were in fact witnessing a migration of Demoiselles through the valley and across the steppes.

Lunch was down by the Orkhon River which had many bare stony islands among the braided channels. I looked in vain for Ibisbills, but all we saw was a single Common Tern (Comintern)

<u>F. 25.8.78</u> Karakorum day.

Kite
Demoiselle Cranes. Anthropoides virgo
    14, 30, 60, 120, 300-400.

Long legged Buzzard
? Upland Buzzard
? Common Buzzard .
    Short-toed Lark   flocks of 100 or more
Asian Skylark
Kestrel
Wheatear.
Herring Gull, perhaps 150 seen.
    Pale backed, pink legged. <u>La.vegae</u>?
Magpie
Common Tern. (Cominteen)
Swallow - deep rufous. breeding.
Amur Falcon
Northern Hobby -

Ground Squirrel
    Citellus erythrogenus
or C. undulaters

Flying Grasshoppers
    2 spp-

Clouded Yellow
    Colias murmidone

Nettle
Silverweed
Groundsel
Plantain
Tiny Gentian .
Hairy Deadnettle -

|
Gentian growing on
river bank in flood
plain of Han River
at Karakorum.
(Life size)

Amur Falcon
<u>Falco vespertinus amurensis</u>

Swallows
at Karakorum .

and a single Magpie, plus a few choughs passing along the slope on the far side. Lots of kites and Ravens in the village.

Stone tortoise at Karakorum

After lunch to the lamasery (euphemistically the museum) which is surrounded by a white wall with 108 (magic Buddhist number) towers – very beautiful. It was built at the end of the 16th century. We smelled incense in the 'museum', clearly indicating that some worship, no doubt clandestine, was still going on. Outside Swallows had cinnamon breasts, and were flying in and out of some of the small buildings where they had nests.

On the way over we had seen a group of 15–20 small falcons using the power lines as a vantage point for catching grasshoppers. They were in nearly the same place on the way back and we managed to get the bus stopped to look at them though they were mostly against the light on the wires – some eating flightless grasshoppers. The first I looked at (from behind) had red eyelids, chestnut thighs and thin vermiculated dark barring on the wings and back. I thought it was a Red-footed Falcon but later I became convinced that it was the Amur Falcon, *Falco amurensis* (or *F. vespertinus amurensis*). Another seemed slightly larger and very like a Hobby with yellow cere, eyelids and legs. It could (must) have been *F. subbuteo*, the Hobby or Northern Hobby. It was a pity not to have longer to watch them, but it was quite a memorable encounter.

After dinner I gave a half hour talk in the big *ger*.

SATURDAY 26 AUGUST

Arrived back in Ulan Bator at 1000 from Khujirt. It was clearly too much to hope that an arrangement would have been made for me to meet a Mongolian zoologist. We had been told that Dr Tsevegmid was away for the whole of August and it is probable that there are no others of his calibre in Mongolia. I had indicated to Khokhoo (our guide) that it would be bad for Mongolian prestige abroad if I had to say that I had not been allowed to meet any scientists, and I think she had taken the point. On the other hand we had given no advance notice of our coming to Ulan Bator and government clearance for Mongolians to meet us obviously takes time in a Communist country.

After lunch Khokhoo came up to me and explained that I wouldn't be able to meet any scientists but that she had arranged for me to visit the State Central Museum which I wanted to do in order to browse and collect names from those jaded and moth-eaten skins that were recognizable and labelled (in most cases with long out-dated scientific names).

Melanocorypha mongolica

I had about an hour in which to go round picking out plants and animals that we'd seen and getting down the scientific names. There was one bird which appeared in two dioramas and also on the shelves of stuffed passerines. It was labelled *Melanocorypha mongolica* but I was quite unable to discover whether it was a large finch or a lark or a large bunting or none of these. It had white secondaries, an incomplete black collar, chestnut cheeks and some white in the tail. It evidently nested on cliffs. [It was the Mongolian Lark.] On several occasions I had seen birds with prominent white in the wings: maybe *M. mongolica*?

I stayed a little too long in the museum and then walked briskly back across the main square to the 1530 rendezvous with the British *chargé d'affaires* who would take Phil and me from the hotel to tea. As I walked along the last stretch to the hotel the Embassy Ford Granada, sporting the Union Flag, came towards me with the Morgans and Phil in it – the *chargé d'affaires* himself at the wheel. I was whisked into the front seat and away we went to the Embassy.

There was a nice tea with scones. Peter Morgan was interesting about the impossibility of getting a reply on paper from the Mongolian Government on any subject whatever. One of the two Siamese cats was sick on the carpet.

SUNDAY 27 AUGUST

Departure from Ulan Bator to Peking by the International Train – due at 0930 from Moscow but $1\frac{1}{2}$ hours late. The bus took us down to the station where we met the Morgans with the Queen's Messengers, and the Japanese Ambassador, Mr Akiyama, with his family. His wife and one daughter were travelling on the train. Mrs A is quite charming (and plays the piano).

To occupy the delay time the bus took us back to the hotel via the main square where a military parade was taking place. It involved a military band, some speech making and the handing out of badges or insignia to individual soldiers who were, we were told afterwards, recruits. There were few spectators but those there wore colourful clothes – the women that's to say.

We all walked across the square and many of the group began taking photographs. Evelyn [Dees] wanted Phil to take her picture with the soldiers in the background. So far no one in authority took much notice, then a blue-uniformed 'policeman' or militiaman began clearly telling us to stop. Eventually he asked the crowd if any one spoke English and a young man said in impeccable English, 'You see, this is not a time to take pictures – it is not allowed'.

We retired across the square, photographing the Sukhe Bator equestrian statue in the middle. Then briefly to the hotel for the facilities and back to the station, where the story was that the train would not come until 1120 or 1130. However at 1100 it came in.

Then followed a scene of indescribable chaos. A crowd of 20–30 people laid seige to the entrances of the 10 coaches. Khokhoo and Edie were quite unable to find out which, if any, compartments had been reserved for us and sleeping car attendants simply blocked all access to the train. We had two young boys as porters for the group's baggage and at last they were allowed to get it into the corridor of Coach No. 7. Poor Khokhoo was losing a lot of face and she castigated the Chinese attendants in their own language.

For a period it looked as if the train would start without us. But as soon as the luggage was on we could all claim the urgency of being on with it, so we were allowed to scramble in. Maybe we were unnecessarily precipitate, but the language problem and some confusion about soft berths which had been paid for by Lindblad Travel, and the 'hard berths' which were all that seemed to be available – though they were perfectly comfortable – all added to the general disorder. There were in fact several minutes before the train started and when it did Edie and I set off along the corridor to find accommodation for all of us. One group of 12 had got in first and were installed in neighbouring hard berth compartments. Our exploration found one (or perhaps two) soft berth compartments and up to three hard berth ones – space for a further 16 had we needed all of it.

Edie tried to work out a plan to suit everyone but she was anxious for Mary Baker, who has been quite ill, not to have to walk a long way along the corridor. Would one couple of our party be prepared to change? This provoked a shocking outburst from our most difficult lady who said she was sick and tired of being told what to do. She and her husband were first in the compartment and had stowed their baggage and they weren't moving. Her husband was greatly embarrassed, not for the first time, by his stupid spoilt wife. I suggested that if we all carried the Bakers' baggage Mary could probably make it and the compartment would be a soft berth one which would be more comfortable for her. Edie accepted the solution, but the eight or nine of us who heard the outburst were confirmed in our conviction that it had been made by a foolish and selfish woman. However we had no difficulty in finding enough people to carry the Bakers' bags along the corridor from Coach 7 to Coach 3 inclusive, that is through five coaches. With these traumatic happenings we were embarked on the 30-hour journey to Peking.

We reached the border at midnight and the Mongolian authorities came to our compartment door for passports and health certificates. Then came more – customs. 'Films,' said one and took a film out of his pocket to demonstrate. His manner was menacing. Phil and Bob Abington got their cameras out and rolled back the film to take it out. Bob's was an Instamatic and had all his shots of the Horse Farm and Karakorum. Luckily Phil's only started at Ulan Bator when the bus went back to the hotel stopping at the main square for the parade.

The Customs Officer turned to me, 'Films'. I gestured that I had none. 'Books,' he said and pointed to my open briefcase from which I had lately produced the passports. There were two printed books: *Field Guide to the Birds of South East Asia* and *Birds of Hong Kong*. He looked through them, then motioned that he wanted to see this diary which he looked through – then the swan booklets and *Guide to Slimbridge*. He made a separate pile of some, including this diary, which suggested he might be planning to confiscate them. He found the envelope full of black and white pictures of Slimbridge, Caerlaverock etc and went through every one, taking them in twos and therefore muddling the order. During all this not a muscle of his face moved. Suddenly he seemed satisfied and turned to Bob, 'Book'. Bob passed his whodunit down. Then they turned to go. Outside the officer took the two films out of his pocket and wrote the number of the compartment on them. His assistant lifted the grille in the corridor covering the heating pipes but found nothing underneath.

I went out to compare notes with the four in the next compartment; they had taken films from three. After a while I decided to walk through to Edie's compartment to see what had happened at that end and to report what had happened to us. I had some difficulty getting back through the train because the officers were still in the corridors, but I arrived in time to receive my passport and to hear that Bob and Phil's films had not been returned though others had. In all six films were confiscated and only two returned.

We spent a lot of time speculating on why this harassment should take place. Had the message come down the line that the tourist group had been photographing military activities? Would they come back and search the rest of our baggage? What was the object of examining our books? Had someone observed me taking notes in this diary? We shall probably never know, but the best guess is that they were simply doing a sample check which no doubt takes place with regularity.

When the train steamed off down to the Chinese border we knew that we should not get our films back but we also knew that they would not come back and search for the 30 odd films in Phil's suitcase. We were shunted into the shed for the wheel changes from broad to narrow gauge – and slept.

MONDAY 28 AUGUST

Breakfast and lunch in the Chinese Restaurant Car – a remarkable contrast in food and service. But the bird-watching had declined. In the time I spent looking out of the window I only clocked up 8 species, though one was *Falco vespertinus* [Red-footed Falcon], probably the subspecies *amurensis*, and another was a flock of some 20 Lapwings.

And so, about two hours behind schedule, we came down through the Great Wall and the mountain pass out into the plain with its ripe maize and millet, sorghum and kaffir corn.

On the platform of the spotlessly clean station were Miss Ko (pronounced Ker) and Miss Wu, our guides during the first period in Peking, and we soon had the baggage in the special vehicle and were off in the bus. The best news for our flagging spirits was that we were to stay not, as before, in the old and rather crumby Minzu, but in the more up-to-date Peking Hotel where the lifts are more numerous and efficient and the rooms equipped with press-button curtains.

The Chinese dinner was much appreciated.

TUESDAY 29 AUGUST

Morning: a trip in the Underground. We drove to a special entrance for tourists; the Chinese came in at the other end of the platform. We watched a crowded westbound and an even more crowded eastbound train which was taken by many of the Chinese including an old man with a magnificent wispy white beard. Finally a beautiful new train pulled in with prints on the walls and martial music playing – which started before our arrival and stopped when we moved out. We made a brief stop to admire another spotless station. People apparently identify the stations by the colour of the marble facings to the pillars.

Then a bus ride to a shopping area where we were to be shown an air-raid shelter but we were early so we had 15 minutes for shopping and I found a plain notebook to succeed this diary and some *cloisonné* pin trays for presents. Then Miss Wu collected us and a man with a torch led us into a clothing shop. Behind a counter, with a tiled floor space which slid out sideways at the touch of a button, was a downward stairway.

As we went down the steps the door slid back above our heads. 'Twas just like a scene from a movie!' We walked several hundred yards round corners, through chambers with generators and air purifiers and medical equipment. It was all very damp but mostly fairly well lit. Eventually we joined the rest of the group in a large dining room where we were given jasmine tea and a lecture with an illuminated plan of the tunnels. This shelter served one neighbourhood and accommodated 10,000 (together Peking's shelters could hold four million people). It was an 'evacuation centre' from which people could walk 10 kilometres underground to escape contamination from noxious substances. The shelters are built with the volunteer labour of those living in the immediate vicinity.

What are the implications of this? They said they were afraid of an attack by the 'Revisionists in the Kremlin'. They expect a war with Russia in due course, but don't want it yet! Does this mean that when they have a good supply of nuclear weapons they will feel that after the initial exchange more Chinese will be left to crawl out of the shelters than on the other side? And will this make them more ready to press the button first?

Later a farewell party with presents from the group to the incomparable Edie and an excellent dinner thereafter.

CHAPTER 3

Japan and Onward

DIARY 32   1978

Between the end of our Lindblad tour in China and the beginning
of our next cruising expedition in the *Lindblad Explorer*, which
started in Hong Kong, there were seven days and we had decided,
sometime before, to accept an invitation by the active Japanese
ornithologists, who had founded the Wild Bird Society of Japan,
to visit Tokyo in order to promote bird conservation. Our hosts
were to be the society and the three people most closely involved
with the visit were its Executive Director Noritaka Ichida, its
Research Director Yozo Tsukamoto, and a member whom I had
met when the *Lindblad Explorer* was in Yokohama a few years
before – a landscape architect named Tsutomu Suzuki. On that
occasion there had been a young swan enthusiast named Kakizawa with him – whom we hoped to meet again and in the event
we did.

WEDNESDAY 30 AUGUST 1978
From Peking it was four and a half hours to Tokyo where we
arrived at 1630 Tokyo time. We landed at Narita Airport – the one
which had the trouble before opening – which is 40 miles from the
centre of Tokyo. The first part of the bus journey went quite fast
through some wooded country and some rice fields where cutting
was just beginning. I saw five species of birds: Jungle Crow (*Corvus
macrorhynchus*), Gray Starling (one big flock on wires and going to
roost in bushes), Tree Sparrow (commonest bird), turtle dove
(probably *Streptopelia orientalis*), and a gull.

But eventually the traffic flow slowed and halted. Progress was
then in brief bursts of forward movement and increasing stationary
periods. It was a full 2 hours before we reached the Tokyo Hilton
Hotel where a room had been booked for us by Lindblad. As I
entered I was immediately recognized by Suzuki and he and
Tsukamoto, and Ichida came eagerly to meet us.

We were very tired and Phil already had the key of our Hilton
room so it took them a little time to persuade us that we should go
with them to the Palace Hotel. But at last we were installed in a
comfortable room and went down to dinner with the three young
men to hear about the programme for the next six days which
sounds eminently reasonable.

THURSDAY 31 AUGUST

I have a slightly turned up tummy so a 0930 start was a welcome change to the pace of Mongolia and China.

At 1000 there was an Audience with HIH Prince Hitachi younger brother of the Crown Prince, whom I had met two years ago in Tokyo and two years before that on his state visit to England.

We drove there – Ichida and I – in the Embassy Jaguar (the Ambassador was using the famous White Rolls). Phil was not invited – (somewhat to the disgust of the WBSJ boys) but this was apparently because the Princess Hitachi was not going to be there.

As we arrived at the smallish villa a man walked up the drive who had been at the meeting two years ago and said in excellent English, 'How nice to see you again'; it was Dr Morioka, Vice-President of the Ornithological Society of Japan. I was ushered to a waiting room and after a while Ichida also came in which was good because he had not been sure he would be allowed to attend the audience.

We were shortly joined by a charming man who spoke excellent English too – Shizuo Saito, special adviser to HIH Prince Hitachi. After some five to ten minutes the Major Domo came in to tell the adviser something. He was in the middle of a long story about his problems in getting into China via Ulan Bator. He finished the story and then said, 'Well the Prince is ready to see us, shall we go in?' We were ushered towards a room with double doors. They were suddenly opened and there was the little Prince all alone and quite close. I had forgotten how small he is. I bowed and then said, 'Imperial Highness, it is so kind of you to come – I mean to allow me to come.' He indicated a seat on his right and we plunged into birds.

The audience was supposed to be half an hour but on the way along the corridor Saito had proposed one hour – and it ran almost to that. Ladies brought tea – and knelt to pour it – and crisp 'cookies'. We covered the travels in this book, the Toki (or Japanese Crested Ibis), *Nipponia nippon* – were there any left in China? – the rare cranes, and the Wildfowl Trust.

Hitachi is not very fluent in English. He wore no glasses (but maybe contacts). His eyes are very narrow slits, which makes him almost totally 'inscrutable'. To my surprise he sent his regards to Phil at the end, which suggested that our enquiry about her attendance at the audience had reached him.

Lunch with Her Britannic Majesty's Ambassador, Sir Michael Wilford – informal and delightful. Afterwards to the Environment Ministry to see the Minister – the Honourable Hisanari Yamada – who had once been a junior diplomat in London. It seemed to go quite well and we were given an undertaking that Japan would *very* shortly ratify the Ramsar Convention [on wetlands of international importance especially as waterfowl habitats]. The position with CITES [Convention on International Trade in Endangered Species] was 'still being examined'.

Great Knot
Calidris tenuirostris
Kasai
2nd Sept 1978
Intermediate plumage.

FRIDAY I SEPTEMBER

Shopping in the morning involved driving through the city for an hour to a special shop to get camera equipment for Phil, binoculars for us both and digital alarm clocks as presents. Our guide was Ranko Lui – a delightful young Japanese girl who acts as a city guide for tourists, but is also a member of the Wild Bird Society of Japan.

In the afternoon there was a symposium on Waterfowl Conservation attended by about 40 people. There were two speeches of welcome – by Mr Matsuda of the WBSJ and Mr Nobe of the Wildlife Protection Section of the Environmental Agency's Nature Conservation Bureau. These were followed by a rather long introduction of me by my old friend Dr Yamashina of the Yamashina Institute for Ornithology. My talk with slides seemed to go down fairly well. At question time I was asked about Wildfowl Trust membership figures, how many geese could be seen by visitors to Slimbridge, the desirability of feeding wild birds as part of a management policy and so on. I said I thought artificial feeding *could* be justified as a part of conservation policy – it was important for education and public awareness. If the ecosystem was altered by it, the gains justified it.

Boat Trip. Sat 2nd Sept.

a.m. **Kasai** The Hon Y. Udagawa
by boat (a very Assemblyman. Tokyo Metro. Govt
handsome launch) T. Hiwatashi. Chief. Marine Park Sect.

Points for Assemblyman Udagawa: (with white hat)
- ▫ Birds as a cultural heritage.
- ▫ Education. School Parties. Hides & covered approach
- ▫ Amount of public use. Public access control.
- ▫ Design Stage details. | Lunch in Museum of Maritime Science.

p.m. Dai-nana Bird Sanctuary & Environs.

A day of AMAZING bird watching in the City of Tokyo.

a.m. Boat Trip & Kasai	p.m. Nr Dai-Nana Sanctuary	In Dai-Nana
• Blacktailed Gull.	Spotbilled Duck	(Common Sandpiper)
Little Egret	Pintail	(Little Ringed Plover)
Great Egret	Shoveler	(Greenshank)
Scaup	Garganey	• Long-toed Stint
Turnstone	(Greenwinged Teal)	• Least Bittern
• Wandering Tattler	Scaup	50 Grey Starling
Herring Gull	(Little Egret)	50 White Wagtail
Great Cormorant	(Great White Egret)	(Little Tern)
Grey Heron	← Night Heron.	Tree Sparrow.
10 Common Tern	30 Ruff	52 Bull-headed Shrike.
Little Tern	30 Red necked Phalarope.	
• Kentish Plover	Wood Sandpiper	52 spp.
• Mongolian Sand Plover	• Broad-billed Sandpiper	
Bar-tailed Godwit.	• Terek Sandpiper	
• Rufous-necked Stint	• Marsh Sandpiper	
Lesser Golden Plover	Greenshank	
Grey Plover	• Latham's Snipe	
• Great Knot	• Dusky Redshank	
• Sanderling	• Curlew Sandpiper	
20 Common Sandpiper.	40 Black-Tailed Godwit	
Green winged Teal.	40 Little Ringed Plover.	
Velvet Scoter.	• Little Stint	
	(Mongolian Sand Plover)	
	Moorhen — Coot	
	Little Grebe.	
	(Little Tern)	
	(Black-tailed Gull)	
	(Grey Heron)	
	Swallow	
	40 Sand martin	

SATURDAY 2 SEPTEMBER

Bird-watching in Tokyo Bay which was amazingly good. Kasai is a man-made estuary with sand flats and there I saw my first Great Knots – *Calidris tenuirostris*. After lunch we went to a small fresh-water marsh with a gravel road along one side – lined with Japanese bird watchers, most of them with telescopes on tripods. This was where we hoped to see a rare wader which had been there for several days – a Siberian Dowitcher, *Limnodromus semipalmatus* – but it was not around today. However there were Chinese Spot-billed Ducks, Common Teal, shovelers, egrets (two sizes) and many waders including Terek and Broad-billed Sandpipers.

The last of our Tokyo bird-watching was at a bird sanctuary, made by the Wild Bird Society, called Dai-nana. It was a very small pond surrounded by trees and did not hold many birds, but there were a few Greenshank, an immature Yellow Bittern, *Ixobrychus sinensis*, and a Bull-headed Shrike, *Lanius bucephalus*.

SUNDAY 3 SEPTEMBER

A rest day. Phil walked round the Imperial Palace Moat which took her $1\frac{1}{4}$ hours. Our hotel overlooks the moat which has small floating platforms for the swans and ducks to climb onto. A terrapin climbed onto one of these and surprisingly turned out to be a Red-eyed

Broadbilled Sandpiper
Limicola falcinellus

Near Dai-nana
2nd Sept. 1978

Terek Sandpiper
Xenus cinereus

Near Dai-nana
2nd Sept 1978

Turtle or Cumberland Terrapin, *Graptemys scripta elegans*, a native of North America. Presumably it had been imported and released into the moat. Also on the moat were several Dabchicks; I painted one which was still in its summer plumage. We had a rather late dinner which turned out to be a mistake as it gave both of us indigestion!

MONDAY 4 SEPTEMBER

Grey day. Hot and humid. Phil and I went with Tsukamoto and Ichida to the Crown Prince's Palace. He was receiving all the volunteer gardeners (men and women) which he does every year. There must have been nearly 100 and we saw them leaving.

We asked if Tsukamoto and Ichida could come in too, but the Chamberlain said 'if only they'd known beforehand . . .'. We were received in the same room as I was received in two years ago, but this time the fishes were different – two species of fresh water gobies – and the Crown Princess was there – and as charming as ever.

Little Grebe
Podiceps ruficollis

In the moat of the Imperial Palace, Tokyo
3rd September 1978.

85

We had half an hour – showed them some photos, ate some sweet cakes, drank green tea, gave HIH Prince Akihito a swan tie and took our leave. All very pleasant and civilized. When it came to choosing a tie, the Crown Princess made the decision.

In the afternoon we called on the Governor of Tokyo – The Honourable Ryookichi Minobe – a rather professorial academic type to look at – and in manner. The meeting had been arranged by the Wild Bird Society and the Governor listened carefully to the points I made: birds are an important Japanese cultural heritage and they lend themselves to study which should be used for teaching in schools. I explained the principle of observation hides and screened approaches. The opportunity was wide open for Tokyo to have the finest urban bird parks in the world, which could be a reality at the stroke of a pen. I told him that we had seen 53 species of birds in 3 hours of bird-watching on Saturday – all within the city limits. Kasai was 35 hectares, a man-made sand flat that was unique – the first in the world, for which he and the city were greatly to be congratulated. Dai-nana was only 3 hectares and *should* be 50 hectares. I wonder how much success I had. It will be interesting to see whether there is any urban bird-watching in Tokyo in ten years' time.

TUESDAY 5 SEPTEMBER

A day at the Tokyo Zoo (Oeno) with Suzuki San* and Kakizawa San, the young swan enthusiast we had met in Yokohama in 1976. The Giant Pandas appeared in good health but most of the cages looked distressingly small to us. The aquarium was excellent.

WEDNESDAY 6 SEPTEMBER

Left Tokyo and arrived in Hong Kong. We found the *Lindblad Explorer* at the Ocean Terminal and installed ourselves in our usual cabin. The cruise begins tomorrow.

THURSDAY 7 SEPTEMBER

We went ashore for lunch at Government House. After the air-conditioning of Government House it was very hot when Phil and I crossed the road opposite to walk up into the Botanical Gardens. We only had time to look at the birds. There were 2 young flamingos of the year – the adults were Greaters and Caribbeans. In the same enclosure were a pair of Red-breasted Geese and a single Ne-ne. Another enclosure had a lovely pair of Jabiru Storks. Others had a flock of Chilean Flamingos, Black-necked Swans and quite a lot of ducks. There were half a dozen aviaries which were most beautifully kept and the birds looked in perfect condition. The labelling was quite good – though not very informative or educational.

Ship sailed at 1700 for Manila.

* First names are not used much in Japan so most people are called by their surname with the addition of San (Mr) after their name.

86

P.S.

Immature Yellow Bittern   (Yoshi goi)
        Ixobrychus sinensis

Dai-nana Bird Sanctuary
Tokyo 2nd September 1978

Bull- headed Shrike
     Lanius bucephalus

Same day, same place

FRIDAY 8 SEPTEMBER

Many thousands of small flying fish of the three species illustrated opposite. The yellow and black-winged one was very handsome.

A Yellow Wagtail was on board all day. (Apparently one was on board soon after departure from Yokohama on 16 August. Some pax seem to think this is the same bird, but others say it was not seen in the interim. The most likely explanation is that two or more wagtails had used the ship as a resting point.) Today's one was very tame – walking up to within a few inches of my foot. It had a few dim dusky spots on the upper breast indicating that it was a young bird of the year. The cheek patch was bluish grey.

Our old friend Tom Ritchie (who has been with us on previous expeditions) gave a morning lecture on sea birds with slides – very well done. He has a very attractive personality. I did an introduction to coral reef fishes illustrated with Phil's pictures of my drawings. The talk, as usual, was a little too long.

We were invited to dinner with the new Captain – Lars Erik Grandguist. During drinks in the lounge disaster struck as I was sucking the lime quarter from my vodka and tonic. The skin was tough and I bit into it. There was a crack and my left upper incisor broke off short at the gum. It is a dead tooth which has been due for a porcelain cap for some time. I repaired to the cabin and quickly discovered that the tooth was not repairable. I had a big black gap and the only way it could be remedied for the moment was to give up smiling.

We should arrive in Manila next day but it would be Saturday. What chances of finding a dentist who could deal with my situation? Future prospects were not much better.

SATURDAY 9 SEPTEMBER

For most of the morning the island of Luzon was passing on the port side a few miles away. At lunch time we passed between Corregidor and the mainland of Luzon, and entered Manila Harbour during a thunderstorm. Mike McDowell – who is a *very* good Cruise Director/Expedition Leader – had radio communication with the agent and asked for a dentist –, and when the agent came on board I was driven in a small jeep through the city to a small street. It was to be a lady dentist and she would treat me in her home.

Dr Loreta Cortes Agaton lives at 1058 Sylvia Street, Ermita, Metro Manila, where she has her 'Clinic' – on the ground floor of a tiny house. When I told her my problem and showed her the broken tooth she laughed and laughed. Then she explained that in the available time there was no chance of a porcelain capping operation which would require X-rays of the root and a period for preparing the porcelain, but that she could make a plate – 'a partial denture' to fill the gap, and in two days I should be quite happy with it. I was to come back at 1830 when the various impressions she had taken

12

8th Sept.

3 species of
Flying Fish

Exocoetus sp

Cypsilurus sp

Hirundichthys
oxycephalus

Fodiator sp

Immature Yellow Wagtail
Motacilla flava ? ssp.
which came on board the
Lindblad Explorer.
8th September 1978

in wax would have been translated into a finished article which would take only 20 minutes to fit and adjust.

I returned to the ship for a couple of hours, bought an embroidered silk evening shirt from the vendors who set up shop at the reception desk, and did some more painting in this book. At 1800 Phil came back from the city tour (mostly shopping) and at 1815 I set off again for Sylvia Street. The clinic was occupied by another patient, so husband Rodolfo offered me a Scotch on the rocks (which I accepted) and a paper to read.

When my turn came, Dr Loreta produced my first plate, and after shaping the incisor to match its neighbour, she fitted it. The cost, ascertained at the first session, was US$60, and I walked out 'wearing' it – if that's the right verb.

Back at the ship people were boarding the buses for the 'Festival Dinner' at the Manila Hotel (in the Penthouse of which General MacArthur lived and worked in World War II).

I changed into my new bought shirt and we caught the last bus. Parts of the evening were enjoyable with some good food and some very high quality dancing, especially by one young man whose performance in two dances (one as a bird) was nothing less than brilliant.

My evening however was overshadowed by the large lump of plastic in my mouth and the difficulty of distinguishing between the edible and inedible elements of the mouthful. Phil was absolutely marvellous at maintaining my morale and her sympathy and understanding made the evening even at times enjoyable. What a fantastically wonderful wife to have!

SUNDAY 10 SEPTEMBER

Manila. Early morning – a grey day, even Grade B – raining. But the sun came out later. The city tour was pretty boring. I don't care much for cities, and this morning I wasn't caring much for anything except the discomfort of my plate. It is extraordinary that such a minor problem (no pain, no outward appearance, a nothing really) can affect one's psychological state so profoundly. Well, the lady said it would take two days to get used to, and I haven't been wearing it for 24 hours.

We sailed for Corregidor at 1300. Phil had a bad tummy and at first decided not to come ashore. I went on and we had a wet landing – the first zodiac landing for these passengers – which turned out to be very wet indeed.

Then Phil arrived with a plan to go bird watching rather than go in the buses. The tour was of the immensely gloomy ruins of the World War II batteries and the huge barracks which are being over-grown by the forest which was replanted in 1947. All these are eerie places with the exception of the war memorial – a rather impressive architectural concept dominated by a fine piece of sculpture latticed against the sky. Some birds here including Green-winged Pigeon and Pied Triller. On the whole though Corregidor is an oppressively sinister place.

I wished I had stayed with Phil and the birds. She saw quite a few, including a good view of a Black-naped Oriole hopping along the ground. When she embarked on the zodiac it was hit by a big wave. There were only four people on board including one of the officers who is very large. The boat was swung sideways and every-one fell – the large officer, the Chief Engineer and Eloff on top of Phil, damaging her left arm and spine. When I got back to the ship she met me at the top of the ladder; she had some pain in her shoulder and three fingers of her left hand had pins and needles. It had almost paralysed her arm to begin with, so that she thought it was broken. Her stiffness made sleeping difficult that night.

Puerto Galera, Mindoro

MONDAY 11 SEPTEMBER
Puerto Galera, Mindoro. A splendid day of snorkelling and SCUBA diving. Three swims. 1 hour snorkelling in the harbour: 61 species. One hour SCUBA to 60 feet, 23 more species. 1½ hours snorkelling after lunch at the first place: 30 more species equals 114 species.

Special delights – *Aeoliscus strigatus* (Shrimpfish or Razorfish) and a *Chaetodon* species new to me: *C. selene*. There was a large scorpaenid which moved towards cover by crawling with its pelvics. (It showed red patches on its pectorals when I got too close. There were 'feathery' patterns across its eyes.) A colony of small *Dascyllus reticulatus* thick over a coral head. A mangrove root with two species of apogons, a shoal of Scats and a baby Mangrove Snapper.

TUESDAY 12 SEPTEMBER

Panay, docked in Iloilo. Bus to lunch at the Anhawa Beach Resort 12 kilometres out of the city. A good lunch with various local fruits including guavas, star fruit, three kinds of bananas and lanzoni (delicious).

A black sand beach with a stiff sea breeze. Thereafter a bus drive to Tigbuan and then the long drive back to Iloilo with a stop at a small clothing shop which had a couple of looms on the ground floor. This was certainly not the thriving cottage weaving industry we had been led to expect. The goods had clearly been bought in for the occasion. Later the buses stopped at a shell shop which used a local translucent oyster shell to make lampshades etc (all fairly dreadful). In retrospect the nicest thing about Iloilo was the friendliness of the people, especially the school children.

The bird list was extremely short: Little Tern, Dollar Bird, Wood Swallow, and Tree Sparrow.

THURSDAY 14 SEPTEMBER

My 69th birthday. 1000 lecture – Wildfowl Trust, with Phil's pictures. 1400 arrived Zamboanga, Mindanao. Phil and I walked

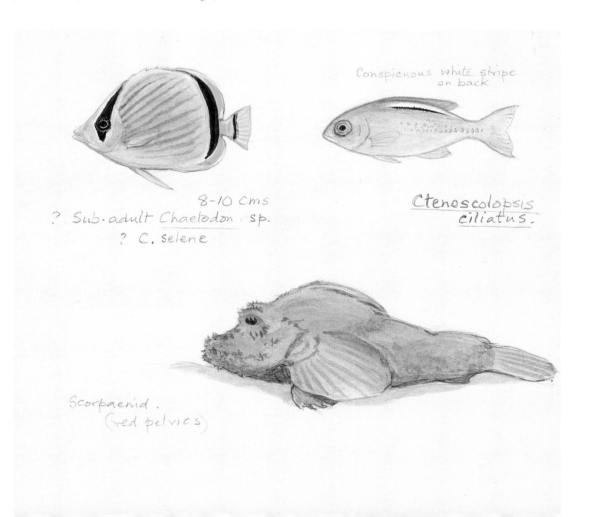

Conspicuous white stripe on back

8-10 cms
? Sub-adult Chaetodon sp.
? C. selene

Ctenoscolopsis ciliatus.

Scorpaenid.
(red pelvics)

<u>Wed. 13th Sept</u>. Arrived before midnight at Sicogon Island (off Pana
moved during breakfast to the opposite side. A very pretty isla
A fairly unspoiled village. Birds near the beach:

  Pacific Swallow. <u>Hirundo tahitica javanica</u>
  Philippine Glossy Starling. <u>Aplonis panayensis</u>
                       with grown young.
  Brown Shrike. <u>Lanius cristatus</u>
  (Yellow-vented Bulbul. <u>Pycnonotus g. goiavier</u>) ??
  Philippine Bulbul. <u>Microscelis ~~gularis~~ gularis guimarens</u>
  Dollar Bird. <u>Eurystomus o. orientalis</u>
  Tree Sparrow <u>Passer montanus</u>
  Parakeet? Guaiabero. <u>Bolbopsittacus lunulatus</u>.
     ~~Sunbird~~

<u>Scuba Dive</u>. c. 1 hr 30 mins. on coast of small island 2 mil
  north of east side village. Water rather murky.
  Species not recorded at Puerto Galera, Mindoro

<u>Chaetodon octofasciatus</u>. v. common
(<u>C. adiergastos</u>) Jim Snyder.
<u>Coradion altivelis</u>. 2
<u>Chelmon rostratus</u>. a few pairs
<u>Heniochus acuminatus</u>. 1
<u>Amphiprion percula or ocellaris</u> ?
(<u>A. frenatus</u>)
(<u>A. clarki</u>)
<u>Diploprion bifasciatum</u>
<u>Cephalopholis</u> sp.
<u>Scolopsis</u> sp
~~Amphiprion~~
<u>Abudefduf sordidus</u>
(<u>Chaetodontoplus mesoleucus</u>) v. common.
<u>Plotosus anguillaris</u>
<u>Lycodontis favagineus</u>. White Moray with black spots
<u>Diademichthys lineatus</u>
        small & wriggly.
(<u>Lutjanus kasmira</u>) Jim Snyder. (<u>Amphiprion perideraion</u>) Jim Snyder

Diademichthys
lineatus
swimming away from
its Sea-urchin
Diadema setosun
in free swimming
colouration.

Late for lunch ashore with hot crab (served by Maggie Fried)

Snorkelling with Phil after lunch in murky water with
some coral & some sand. <u>Upside-down jellyfish</u> in the shallows.

Therapon jarbua   1
Upeneus tragula   2 
Tiny shoal fish in thousands 
Opisthognathus sp. 
Baby Barracuda 1 
Pterois volitans 1
Pomacentrids. A oxyodon 1
    A. sp. —————————————>
    A. sp ————————————————>

Scolopsis cancellatus 1

Choerodon schoenlini

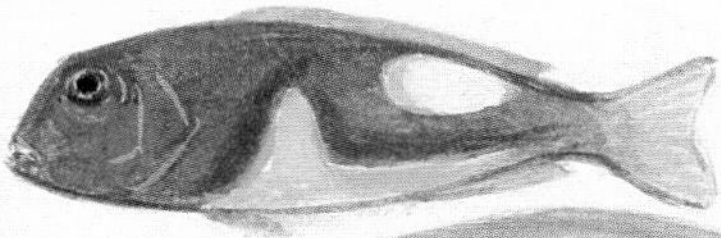

Choerodon sp.

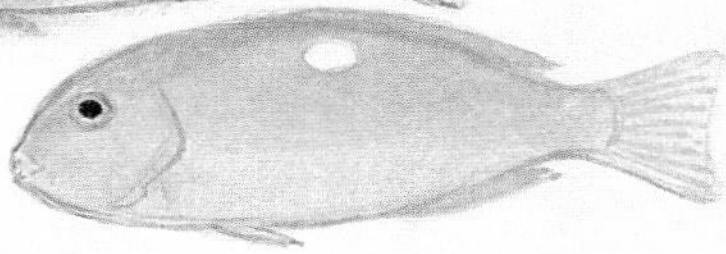

Wrasse
mimicking a
Scolopsis?

      ?

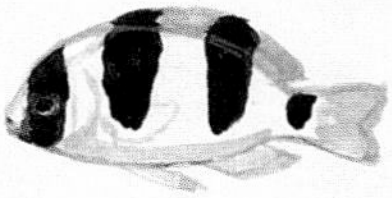

P. annulatus ? Pomacentrid
          mimicking
        Dascyllus melanurus
            + aruanus.

colopsid ?
behaviour.

  ?

rasonet

Cryptocentrus
    sungami
   with pinkish 'pistol shrimp'.

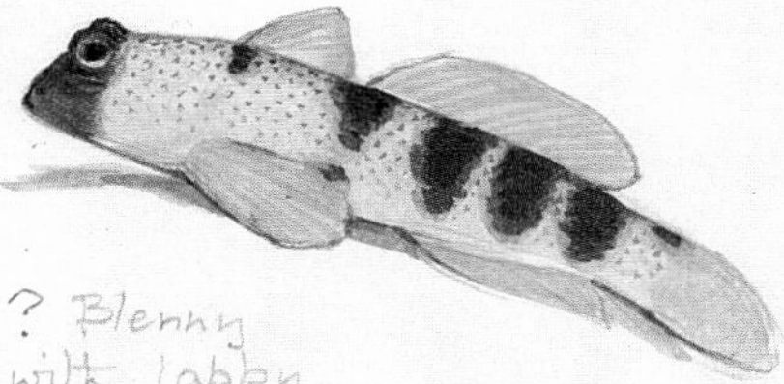

? Blenny
with labby
Sometimes in pairs.

32 new spp

in the city streets in the rain (with shelter from the colourful umbrella Phil gave me this morning as a birthday present). In the evening we all went to the Zamboanga Plaza Hotel for dinner of sea food and fruit – notably ripe mangosteen. The dinner and floorshow didn't last very long so we joined a crew party in the lounge back at the ship. Phil cannot really dance without exacerbating the damage to her arm (and perhaps spine) so she went to bed early. I stayed and danced a little for exercise.

The main features of my birthday were Phil's present of the umbrella, the fact that the audience sang 'happy birthday' at the beginning of my lecture, the special dinner and a number of cards and letters from many friends, crew, staff and passengers. So I had a *very* nice birthday.

SATURDAY 16 SEPTEMBER

The ship sailed into Sandakan Harbour on the north coast of Sabah past the great red cliffs of Berhala Island where a pair of White-breasted Sea Eagles were doing aerobatics. I had a turned-up tummy, and quite a bad overdose of sun on my back.

Just as we were boarding the bus to the Sepilok Orangutan Rehabilitation Centre Stanley de Silva turned up. We have to leave the ship tomorrow so we can go to the General Assembly of the International Union for Conservation of Nature and Natural Resources at Ashkhabad [in the USSR] and Stanley is going to look after us during our short stay in Sabah. He is the Director of the National Parks here [and an old friend from the SSC].

Loto
Young male Orang Utan
Pongo pygmaeus
Sepilok, Sabah, Malaysi

The centre, which was set up by Barbara Harrison, is about fifteen kilometres out of town on the edge of a forest reserve and is very well done on the whole. We saw some captive animals including an Orangutan, young Sun Bears, and a supremely indifferent Clouded Leopard in perfect condition which slept and never woke up for the invasion of 50-odd people.

We moved out over a bridge into the tall forest. 100 yards down a path was the feeding station to which the released Orangutans can return when they wish. At the side of the path was a beautiful green arboreal lizard with movable eye turrets just like those of the *Chamaeleonidae* – a marvellous example of convergent evolution. It had matchstick thin legs, long toes and an immensely long thin tail. He was sitting atop a bush just below eye level.

Near the feeding station were altogether seven – possibly eight – Orangutans including Joan, a mother with tiny baby, who was said to have become aggressive, especially to white women, three of whom she had bitten quite badly. So we were advised not to go too near her. To begin with she was high in a tree but eventually she came down and towards us near the feeding station. However having posed for photographs and picked up some food she went off again, with baby clinging to her side.

Another feature of Sepilok was the butterflies, including a huge 'ghostly' one which flapped very slowly and floated through the forest, and one of the famous leaf butterflies.

Left: Rain forest at Sepilok, Sabah

Right: Baby Orangutan, Sepilok

Back at the ship I skipped lunch and after the others had had it we went off to the 'Kelinik' of Dr Y. K. Chu to get Phil X-rayed. He was a nice young man who seemed medically quite alert.

Stanley de Silva and I sat in the hot little waiting room below while Phil and Ralph [Wilson, Dr] went upstairs to the radiographer. It was very hot in the waiting room and my intestinal spasms were rather bad. I went along to the primitive 'hole-in-floor' loo (which had no paper) to no avail, and went back to the waiting room, now rather crowded and very hot. I was sweating profusely. Then Phil and Ralph reappeared. The X-ray showed a cracked rib. No wonder she had been in pain for almost a week since the accident in the zodiac in Corregidor.

I was feeling very weak and faint. I put my head between my knees and Ralph felt my pulse which was barely detectable. The bench in the waiting room was cleared so that I could lie down; I never lost consciousness quite, but I was only just there. Ralph said my pulse was coming back quite well. Dr Chu said he had a room I could lie down in, but de Silva had gone to bring the Land Rover from the car park and Ralph thought it best to get me back to the ship. So I was helped out to the car. We wondered afterwards what the other patients thought of someone taken ill in the waiting room being whisked away from the ministrations of Dr Chu and hoped it would not affect his custom.

By the time we got back to the ship I was feeling a good deal better and was able to walk on board unaided. Lying down in the cabin I felt fairly normal again though the spasmodic tummy pains continued and Ralph brought me all kinds of pills to deal with them.

It still remains a little obscure what caused my heart to stop pumping enough blood to my head. Was it the gastroenteritis? Was it the over exposure to the sun which I had foolishly allowed in Santa Cruz Island and which was producing a throbbing under the red skin of my back and the backs of my legs? Was it a complaint by my heart that I had been over exerting it during the SCUBA diving? We may never know, but it was an unnerving experience, and perhaps also a warning not to push all these things forward *too* ambitiously!

SUNDAY 17 SEPTEMBER

A morning of packing for me. It turned into an emotional morning for we left the ship a few minutes before her 1.00 pm departure. The level of affectionate feelings from everyone – crew and passengers, especially the crew – was extremely heartwarming, but at times almost overwhelming.

Later we moved in to the Sabah Hotel, Sandakan.

MONDAY 18 SEPTEMBER

A second trip out to Sepilok with a visit to the Forestry Research Centre to identify insects we have been seeing.

By boat with Stanley de Silva to the Turtle Islands about 35 miles from Sandakan. First stop – Little Bakkungaan. After installing our gear in the small house on stilts Phil and I had a walk among the coconut palms, finding a marvellous deep scarlet dragonfly which Phil photographed. We got very hot, came back and went swimming off the beach for 1 hour. 57 species. Rather murky and mostly dead coral.

In the afternoon an abortive effort to find better coral in a metal dinghy with outboard motor. The 'reef' we selected from the chart was all weed. *Acanthurus mata* was the only new fish. The boat trip was bad for Phil's stretched arm nerves and cracked rib, especially on the return trip against the wind. I should have realized this and not embarked on it at all.

Back on the porch of the house on Little Bakkungaan we watched a White-bellied Sea Eagle bring a crab to the top of a decapitated palm tree and eat it. It looked like an extraordinary balancing act.

Meals are from tins and frugal. After supper the warden, Idrus (Eye-drus), came to say that a turtle had come up onto the beach. It was a very large female Green Turtle and was laying when we got there. A second one was laying about 10 yards away. By torch light we watched the eggs plopping down into the sand pit. The big female was unmarked and had to be tagged when she had finished

The *Lindblad Explorer* sailing away, Sandakan

The Turtle Islands of Sabah

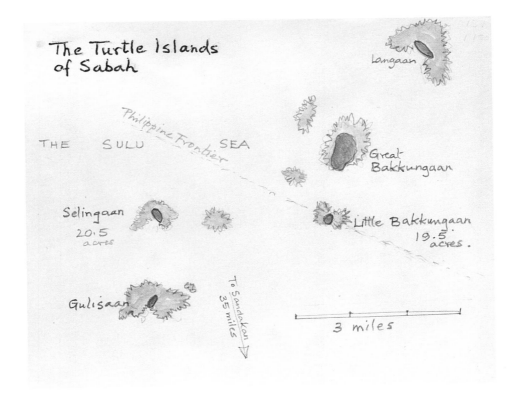

THE   SULU   *Philippine Frontier* SEA

Langaan

Great Bakkungaan

Little Bakkungaan
19.5 acres.

Selingaan
20.5 acres

Gulisaan

To Sandakan 35 miles

|——————|————|————|
3 miles

Little Bakkungaan.   Warden: Idrus Chung.   19.9.78

Collared Kingfisher
Wood Swallow.
Drongo, Bronzed.
Yellow-vented Bulbul
Yellow-bellied Sunbird.
Warbler ? sp.
Chestnut Munia.
White breasted Sea Eagle.

Morning Swim.
Dead coral at high water.
Rather murky   57 spp.

Afternoon short swim on reef
between Selingaan & Little Bak.
Murky — all weed. No good at all.

(Wed 20. cont)

laying; the smaller female was already tagged. I was surprised that the females themselves were down about a foot or 18 inches below the level of the beach when laying. Later we found another female still digging. After watching both females engaged in the laborious 'infilling' process we set off back to bed.

The hatchery where the turtle eggs were reburied

There was a bright moon, and it was all very beautiful. Passing the hatchery (to which the eggs are moved and reburied in a fenced enclosure, each clutch inside its own circle of wire netting) we decided to go in and see whether any broods were hatching. In the centre of each wire cylinder was a marker peg of split bamboo. In one of them was something dark as well. The torch revealed that it was a baby turtle half out of the sand. A second one's flipper was showing. We looked at the first baby and were moving on when suddenly I noticed that where there had been only one baby and a flipper above the sand now the whole wire circle looked black. The torch revealed that at least 50 young turtles were now – about one to two minutes after we had found the first one – milling around and over each other in a struggling mass. As we left the hatchery we found another milling mass of at least 70 babies in one of the wire cages. (One of the three wardens on the island would shortly be there with a wire basket with which he would transfer these babies to the beach and so release them into the sea.) It was a deeply impressive phenomenon and we found it most dramatic and exciting – a splendid climax to an excellent day. We slept to the plash of the waves 20 yards from the cabin.

Little Bakkungaan
19.9.78

Warbler with
NO wing bar
whatever.

Immature White-bellied Sea Eagle
<u>Halaeetus leucogaster</u>
with Crab, at sunset.

WEDNESDAY 20 SEPTEMBER

Happily Phil's spine, shoulder and hand took no harm from the bumpy boat trip, though she didn't sleep very well. Another lovely day though with more wind. Idrus told us that six turtles had laid on the beach (there are often many more in August) and seven clutches had hatched in the hatchery. Our big female had laid 118 eggs. Over 600 baby turtles had been released.

After breakfast of pawpaw and crisp bacon, cooked by Stanley, we went out with Idrus to see the extraordinary upwellings of mud at the highest part of the island. There were a dozen or so places with wet clay-filled pools where bubbles were coming up. There was no available explanation of this, but the mud is not hot, so no volcanicity appears to be involved. The grass doesn't grow well round them, suggesting that the water is not fresh, and indeed it tasted salty.

Idrus took us on to see a Collared Kingfisher nest in a burnt palm stump – a surprisingly small hole with 2 feathered young inside.

Back to the 'cabin' where we collected our swimming gear and went to the beach on the lee side, where the turtles hauled out, and on the opposite side from yesterday's swim. The water was still very murky but there was more living coral and therefore many additional fish species – including 7 chaetodons as opposed to the $1\frac{1}{2}$ the day before.

After the swim (we had brought no towels at all!) we packed up

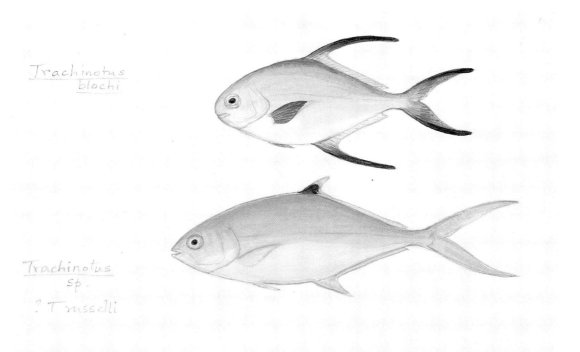

Trachinotus
blochi

Trachinotus
sp.
? T russelli

Hatchling
Green Turtle
Chelonia mydas

and embarked in the launch which took us for an hour to Selingaan Island. We were greeted by the Warden – Richard Yamie – with sparse beard – bright and intelligent. It was very hot indeed, being 1130. We walked up past a hatchery (they have two on this island, so as to be able to rest one each year because of pollution by addled eggs). We saw the Warden's cabin and then went on up the middle of the island to some buildings in process of construction which will be a visitor hostel for 15 people. It was being quite nicely done. There was a pile of sand for making cement in one of the buildings which had rat tracks all over it. The Warden suggested that they were Ant Lion pits! But that was rubbish. Incidentally one turtle had nested directly underneath the Warden's house.

Stanley's Turtle Island 'empire' is impressive. He has, apparently, a good group of men doing the work – collecting and replanting the eggs, counting and releasing the hatchlings, marking the adult turtles. With the exception of a rat problem (notably bad on Selingaan) and the rumoured sale of *some* turtle eggs, the operation seemed to us pretty good. Stanley doesn't snorkel and does require his men to keep him supplied with lobsters – not *quite* right in a national park. But he sees the turtle work as the main and only object of the Park's existence.

I walked back to the boat along the shore where I could distinguish a few fish species we hadn't recorded on this trip: notably *Tylosurus crocodilus* – the needle or gar fish – and a school (probably) of Mullet. There was no time to get a snorkel out.

At 1230 we left in relatively calm weather with bright sun and, after a lunch of bananas, rambutan and tangerine, reached Sandakan at 1405. We were soon installed in Room 12 at the Sabah Hotel, and

Sabah Fruits
~~Lanzak~~.
Langzat

Rambutan

Scarlet-backed
Flowerpeckers displaying
Dicaeum cruentatum.
nigrimentem

Chestnut
Munia
Lonchura

Dusky Munia
Lonchura fuscans

half an hour later the room looked essentially 'lived in': every inch of floor space, chair space and bed space was occupied. The Chinese dinner was memorable: sizzling prawns, sweet and sour pork and flied lice, followed by a big bowl of lychees each. 'What a good dinner!' we said. And it was.

THURSDAY 21 SEPTEMBER

At 1615 a taxi came to take us to the airport for our flight to Kota Kinabalu there to meet the Environment Minister and the Chairman of the National Parks. Stanley flew with us. The plane was half an hour late landing, making us late for the Minister's dinner. Eventually, after a shower in the Shangrila Hotel, we arrived in the Grill Room of the largest and newest hotel in KK and found a party of about a dozen. Although the Minister of the Environment, Yap Pak Leong, was our host, it soon became clear that the Chairman of the National Parks, Tansri (Lord) Jayasuriya – a lawyer said to be the Chief Minister's principal adviser, and a former minister – was the most powerful person present. He was quite young, rather good-looking, and talked all the time, but with quite a responsive intellectual flair. We got on well together and I raised the three main points for discussion (and many more) during preliminary drinks and dinner – which went on till 2330. The points were first the current extensive destruction of the forest by logging in the proposed Sungai Danum National Park, the future of the Sepilok Orangutan Reserve and finally the possibility of some supra-national control of the Turtle Islands to include the nearby Philippine ones as well as the Sabah ones. We also talked about merging the Game Branch of the Forestry Department with the National Parks. It is probably the only way of getting security in the long term for the most important areas.*

Jayasuriya took us back to the hotel in his air-conditioned Mercedes (too cold). The dinner of fried (imported) king prawns had been very indigestible. We finally got to bed at a quarter past midnight and both of us slept poorly. So much for our 'good night's rest' before the long all-night flight to Moscow.

FRIDAY 22 SEPTEMBER

Jayasuriya had arranged a boat trip for me out to some nearby islands – there were only $1\frac{1}{2}$ hours available but I decided to go complete with mask, snorkel, flippers and drawing pad. The water was much clearer than at the Turtle Islands and there was much more living coral, but surprisingly few fish. We went out in a big launch, and came back in a speed boat. (Lesser) Crested Tern and Black-naped Terns.

Then began our desperate journey to Ashkhabad. The first leg

---

* The Sepilok Orangutan Reserve was extended and is still maintained, and so are the Sabah Turtle Islands, but the other points did not come to fruition.

to Singapore by Singapore Airlines was good, with an excellent lunch, preceded by champagne and accompanied by white wine. The new Arrival building at Singapore Airport is very fine and spacious. The Departure building is the old one that we have spent so many hours in waiting for air connections, and this time we had about 3 hours to kill. I spent some of the time buying the pen I am writing this with (advantages of ball-point in these diaries is that it is waterproof and if splashed with rain, effervescent spray from gin and tonic, or plain spit, it doesn't come off on the opposite page as the felt-pen inks do) and some of the time painting up the birds and fishes.

Eventually we could check in for Aeroflot SU560 to Moscow. Phil and I had time to have a gin and tonic, to change our money back, she to buy a book, and lay in some 'iron rations' of chocolate for the USSR. By the time our flight was called we were both feeling pretty jaded. And what a dreadful flight it was! The plane was full. We had seats three rows from the back and were surrounded by very noisy and ultimately very drunk young Asian hoodlums –? Vietnamese. The smell from the toilets, including the pervading smell of Russian disinfectant, was continually wafted out at us.

Phil and I must both have slept a little, but it was extremely cramped. The only good thing about the flight was an absolutely perfect landing in Moscow.

SATURDAY 23 SEPTEMBER

Arrived in Moscow and found our visas were dated 24th! However we were eventually allowed through. David Downing (the new Scientific Attaché) had come to meet us – also Dr Gan and an interpreter from the Ministry of Agriculture. The plane had nearly beaten them all by arriving 25 minutes early! It was 4°C (after about 35°C in Sabah).

A sleep in the morning, and then the Downings called to drive us to the Embassy for lunch with the Ambassador, Sir Curtis Keeble and Scottish wife. Lunch à quatre. We shouldn't have eaten so much and both of us suffered from indigestion caused no doubt at least in part by exhaustion. Nor should we have gone out to dinner but we managed to get away soon after 2200 without having to eat too much; the wine was excellent.

Back to our pokey room (with no ventilation) in the Hotel Rossiya, to pack for a 0700 start on the long flight back to Ashkhabad (a third of the way back to Singapore!).

My tummy was turned up through the night.

MONDAY 25 SEPTEMBER

Arrived at 0100 in Ashkhabad. 0900 chaired SSC meeting.

WEDNESDAY 27 SEPTEMBER

In the afternoon I gave my report on SSC to the General Association.

It went down rather well. There was an important addendum which restated the Union's adherence to the moratorium on all commercial whaling.

THURSDAY 28 SEPTEMBER

Morning. Played hookey from the assembly and went by bus to a gorge – an hour away. Quite an impressive landscape. Spent lunchtime in the Botanic Gardens.

Afternoon devoted to the World Conservation Strategy – technical session. Lee Talbot in the chair.

The WCS, which is being drafted at the IUCN headquarters in Switzerland, is a document for signature by all nations recognizing that, if human development is to be sustainable, it must be linked to the conservation of living resources; the WCS sets out guidelines for how this can be achieved.*

* It was prepared by IUCN with the advice, cooperation and financial assistance of WWF and UNEP and was endorsed by FAO and UNESCO. The strategy was launched in 1980.

Gazella subgutturosa

FRIDAY 29 SEPTEMBER

Morning. Technical Meeting. Detail of the World Conservation Strategy. I spoke on not using MSY [Maximum Sustainable Yield], the calculation of which is likely to be dangerously over-optimistic, and not measuring priorities for endangered species in terms of 'current value, expected value and potential value'.

Salt lakes at Badkhyz from the air

SUNDAY 1 OCTOBER

Early start (0630) for Mary and then Badkhyz. We, the Kuenens, and the Bannikovs flew in a turbo prop. 50 minutes to Mary where we climbed into a very plushy helicopter which took us in an hour like a magic carpet to the Badkhyz Reserve. First we followed the irrigated strip along the Murgab River, then cut across the desert with its patches of burnt grass to the Kyzyl-Djar Gorge. On the eastern lip of the gorge some wild sheep (*Ovis ammon*) were seen from the opposite side of the chopper. Also quite a lot of gazelles, *G. subgutturosa*, and Bannikov saw two Kulan, *Equus hemionus*. On our side was the gorge with steep red cliffs and quite a lot of birds of prey. A Griffon Vulture, *Gyps fulvus*, circled above us, and below was a thermal full of Steppe Eagles with another Griffon among them. The highest hills were about 2,500 feet but we descended into the gorge where it ran out into a wide valley – the Er-Oilan-Duz hollow with a dried-up salt lake and, according to the literature, 'a group of almost black, whimsically arranged hills in and around the salt pan'. These were volcanic extrusions, on which I saw a

109

Steppe Eagle and a large falcon (Saker? Gyr?). We landed here and went for a walk; the most interesting bird was *Podoces panderi*, Pander's Ground Jay.

After 'elevenses' of chicken, cheese, grapes and wine in a tent, back into the helicopter to go to the pistachio savannah near Pul-i-Khatum. On the way we saw 3 pairs of Kulan (Anakr or Onager) and one single one – 7 animals. We were maybe 400 feet above them and they paid little attention to our passage.

Later we enjoyed a four course meal under a pistachio tree with toasts (and toasted pistachio nuts) before returning to Mary by helicopter, then straight into the prop-jet and back to Ashkhabad through a sandstorm with gale force winds.

TUESDAY 3 OCTOBER

In the evening there was a show of Yury Ledin's films. Redbreasts, Polar Bears, Sea Lions and Fur Seals in the Commander Islands. The Polar Bear film is one of the best Natural History films I've ever seen. There is a good story line about taking a captive born 5-weeks-old bear, called Aika, to Novaya Zemblya in an attempt to release it into the wild, the relationship between Aika and Ledin's young daughter, Veronika, the attitudes of a wild mother bear Matilda and her 2 cubs and 2 young but fully grown males. Incredible pix of Polar Bears, also Ivory Gulls. Ledin says he will never believe anyone who claims to have shot a Polar Bear in self defence.

THURSDAY 5 OCTOBER

The Conference has been very positive and the World Conservation Strategy has had an extremely beneficial effect in drawing everyone together into a more purposeful frame of mind. Now we have to convert the strategy into action.

FRIDAY 6 OCTOBER

Awakened at 0400 for homeward flight. Being a Government guest gives us a car to ourselves, whereas often it would be more pleasant to go in the bus. About 30 people were taking the same flight. Of the two unpleasantnesses that have arisen during the conference – the failure of the Soviet organizers to grant visas to the delegates from Israel and South Africa which would allow them to take part in the post-conference study tours, and the persistent threats to the South Korean delegates by the North Koreans (6 against 3), the second came to the fore again, as further midnight threats were made and both before and after the flight there were ugly incidents in which some of the American delegates had physically to shield the South Koreans.

The flight itself, in the analogue of a Boeing 707, took 3 hours and 20 minutes, and was perfectly comfortable, though the food was shocking. Then on back to England.

CHAPTER 4

A Month in Australia and Malaysia

DIARY 34   1979

In April 1979 I was invited to make a whistle-stop tour of Australia to launch the World Wildlife Fund there. Between my arrival in Sydney on 16 April and my departure from the same city on the 27th of the month, I visited in quick succession Melbourne, Adelaide, Perth and Brisbane and saw some rare birds and other animals. I had little time to keep my diary. The saddest part of this gruelling trip was not to have Philippa with me, though she came out to meet me later in Kuala Lumpur for some swimming and filming with Ron and Valerie Taylor on Pulau Redang's coral reefs. Our task was to make an underwater film to help publicize WWF Malaysia.

FRIDAY 13 APRIL 1979
Usual rush to finish letters before 1430 departure from Slimbridge – without my darling Phil, who will be spared the desperate Australian programme and will come out to meet me in two weeks.

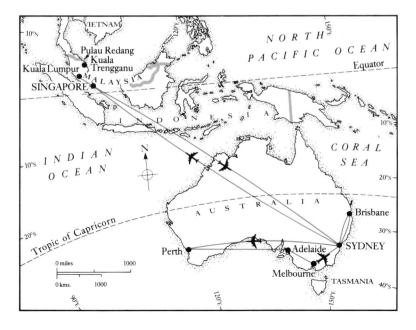

ITINERARY 1979

Fri 13 April. Leave home

Sat 14.   Arr. Kuala Lumpur

Sun 15. Dep. KL

Mon 16. Arr. Sydney 0630
    1930. Trustees Dinner. Opera Ho.
    (0820 Radio) Sydney: Menzies Hotel

Tues 17. 0930 Trustees + AGM WWF
    1230 Rotary Lunch 1015 TV
    1430 Press Conf.
    1630 Barry Cohen Opposition Leader
        Sydney: Menzies Hotel

Wed 18   NSW Premier
    1230 NSW Inst. of Directors
    p.m. Media
    1800 NSW Cons. Groups
    ~~2030 Dep Sydney TA 497~~
    ~~2100 Arr Canberra~~
    ~~Canberra: Lakeside Int. Hotel~~

Thurs 19. ~~0900 Prime Minister~~
    ~~1230 D MEM lunch~~
    ~~pm Gungahlin~~
    ~~1730. Dep Canberra TA 427~~
    ~~1825 Arr Melbourne~~
        Melbourne Hilton

Fri 20 am. Victoria Premier
    1230 Lunch. Inst of Directors
    p.m. Media
    1800 Victoria Cons. Groups.
        Melbourne Hilton

Sat 21
    1845. Dep Melbourne TA 50
    1925 Arr Adelaide
        Gateway Inn

Sun 22
    2000 SA Trustees Dinner
        Adelaide: Gateway Inn

Mon 23 am. SA Premier
    1230. SA Inst of Directors
    p.m. Media
    1800 SA Cons. Groups
    2115 Dep. Adelaide   TA 12
    2245 Arr Perth Parmelia Hilton

Tues 24 am. WA Premier
    1230 Businessmens Lunch.
    pm. Media
    1800 WA Cons Groups.
        Perth: Parmelia Hilton

Wed 25
    1301. Dep Perth TA1.
    2000 Arr Sydney Dep 2030 TA409
    2145 Arr Brisbane: Crest Int Hotel

Thurs 26 a.m. Qld Premier
    1230 Qld Businessmen's Lunch.
    pm Media
    1800 Qld Cons. Groups.
    2030 Qld Trustees Dinner

Fri 27 Apr. 0805 Dep Brisbane TA449
    1000 Arr. Sydney.
    1200 S. Pacific Conference
    1500 Dep. Sydney QF 001
    2240 Arr Kuala Lumpur British H.C.
        Carcosa

Sat 28.
    1735. Phil arrives KL
    2000 St Georges Soc. Dinner.
        KL: High Comm. Carcosa

Sun 29. 0730-1130 Ampang Forest Res.
        H.C. Carcosa

Mon 30 1000 Dep KL
    1105 Arr. Kuala Trengganu
    1200 Lunch Pantai Motel
    1300 Dep. Trengganu for Pulau Redang

Tues 1 May to   } On location at
Sun 6 May   } Pulau Redang.

Mon 7. Dep. Pulau Redang
    Arr. Kuala Trengganu
        Pantai Motel

Tues 8 am. Meeting with Mentri Besar
    or State Sec. Trengganu
    1745 Dep. KT. MH 143
    1850 Arr. K.L.   HC Carcosa

Wed 9   Briefing by Ken Scriven
            HC Carcosa

Thurs 10   Public Holiday
    1130 WWF Trustees Mtg. Lake Club
    1300 Lunch
    1630 TV Interview HC Carcosa

Fri 11   Meeting with Prime Minister
            Datuk Hussein Onn.
    1900 "The Seas Must Live
        at Shell Theatre. Carcosa
            H.C. Carcosa

Sat 12 1000 Min. of Science, Tech + Env.
    Tan Sri Ong Kee Hui
    2000-0100 Turtle Ball
        ? HC Carcosa

Sun 13

    2300 Dep. KL. MH 002

Mon 14 ██ May.
    0935 Arr. London Heathrow.
        Return home.

Last letters involved replies to businessmen prepared to be Patrons of the Wildfowl Trust's £1.6 million Appeal, letters of invitation to new members of the Survival Service Commission's specialist groups, one to Prince Philip about the WWF Presidency and one to Prince Charles about writing to the President of the Ivory Coast on the protection of West African elephants in the Tai National Park.

Mike [Garside] read me letters and papers and took down dictation all the way to London Airport.

But, oh, how I *hate* being without my wonderful Phil. I refuse. . . I positively refuse, to travel without her ever again. If she can't go for any reason, I won't go either.

I watched two films and snatched a couple of hours' sleep before we landed in Kuala Lumpur.

SATURDAY 14 APRIL
A good night's rest at the hotel.

SUNDAY 15 APRIL
Early breakfast – out to Ampong Primary forest and reservoir. 16 species of birds seen or heard. Malay Great Argus heard (2 males). Swiftlets in tunnel. Indian Cuckoo (Beethoven bird). Green Broadbill and 2 barbets heard. No gibbons around. Emperor Cicadas were singing.

Meeting with Robert Oliver and fiancée Virginia. Discussed his problems in establishing the secretariat of the Asian Elephant Group of IUCN's SSC in Sri Lanka. His master plan was apparently lost in

The Emperor Cicada

Ampong - 14.4.79

Life size (approx.)

(Seen through binoculars)

the post so that the Director of Wildlife (Lyn de Alwis) and T. W. Hoffmann, President of the Wildlife and National Parks Society, did not receive them, and regard themselves as slighted – especially Hoffmann who is influential.

Afternoon. Flew out of KL by Malaysian Airlines System to Singapore in order to change to the Qantas flight to Sydney.

I have 10 days in which to tell Australia about WWF – with speeches in Sydney, Melbourne, Adelaide, Perth and Brisbane. It is a daunting programme and a great responsibility. I can only *hope* that WWF Australia will become a reality.

RAW MATERIAL FOR SPEECHES ON AUSTRALIAN TOUR TO
LAUNCH WWF AUSTRALIA

WWF History. Launched in 1961 – 18 years ago. Morges Manifesto. IUCN sister organization. 400 members (governments and NGOs). Network of scientists. SSC: over 1,000 specialists. WWF a new Noah's Ark. Liaison between scientists and fund-raisers (hallmark of joint operations to this day).

Chronological order of formation of National Organizations of WWF: UK, US, Switzerland, Netherlands. Twenty seven NOS now.

How many endangered species? Animals: 1,088 vertebrate species and sub-species listed in SSC's Red Data Books. 321 mammals, 435 birds, 98 reptiles, 40 amphibians, 194 fish. 60% threatened by habitat destruction, 30% threatened by over exploitation. Other threats: introduced species, killing to protect crops or livestock, food supply reduction. Most are threatened in several ways.

Many more invertebrates on critical list: molluscs, crustacea, spiders, butterflies and moths. Also 2,500 species of plants.

2,000 WWF projects undertaken. Endangered species, for example: Tiger, Wolf, Polar Bear, Asiatic Lion, Javan Rhino, Arabian Oryx, Vicuna, Hawaiian Goose, Marine Turtle, Crocodile, Giant Tortoise, Iguana, Devil's Hole Pupfish. All these and many more given a new lease of life by WWF.

260 National Parks and protected areas in five continents. Area: 1,300,000 square kilometres equal to France, West Germany, Italy and UK combined.

Scope. 'The conservation of nature and the natural environment of man in all its forms: fauna, flora, landscape, soil, water, air and other renewable natural resources . . . to create awareness of the threats to nature . . . to generate and attract, on a world-wide basis, the strongest possible moral and financial support for safe-guarding the living world, and to convert such support into actions based on scientific priorities.'

Cost efficiency. Income from endowment funds and commercial activities, such as the 1001 club = $10 million. Royalties from licensing WWF's name and its panda symbol.

Now *100% of donations* received by WWF (International) are

available for conservation projects. *None* is retained for administration.

Conservation is for humans too. Recent studies have shown that the impact of human activities on the biosphere is of such magnitude that unless controlled they must threaten the carrying capacity of the globe for humans. (Pollution, greenhouse effect, cutting down of tropical forest at 50 acres per minute, desertification, etc.)

Treaties and Conventions. For example, agreements affecting polar bears, wetlands, CITES, migratory animals, world heritage.

WWF's *Educational Role*. Getting the message across to the decision-makers of today and tomorrow. Youth Federation for Environmental Studies and Conservation, Wildlife Clubs in Kenya, Zambia, India. In Switzerland 10% of all teachers are WWF members.

Ecosystem Conservation Group. World Conservation Strategy. To promote conservation as *an integral part of sustainable development*.

Rather a traumatic discovery when transferring – with little time to spare at Singapore – that my passport bore *no* Australian Visa. At first, the Chinese girl said there was no way I could get on the plane as the airline would be fined if I went on it without a visa – visas have evidently been needed for three years for anyone staying more than two days. Had I any letter of authorization showing that I was going to visit the Prime Minister, the Governor General? Well, I had my green itinerary. The girl took it away to a telephone and eventually I was led down to the gate by the same girl, still concerned about my address in Australia, and allowed to board the plane – a considerable relief, after the initial diagnosis that I would have to stay in Singapore till Monday to get a visa at the Australian Consulate!

MONDAY 16 APRIL
And so to Sydney where I was met by the WWF team: David Mitchell (PR Director for WWF International), Adrian Stark (Director of WWF Australia) and Barry Cocks, also of WWF (A). There too was my old friend Vincent Serventy – the very distinguished Australian naturalist – whom I had not seen for many years. After some immigration trouble we drove through the empty early-morning streets of Sydney to the Menzies Hotel.

Quiet day with speech writing and some sleep. 1800 briefing by John Cameron, Hon. PR Consultant WWF (A). 1930 WWF Trustees' dinner in the Opera House. I met most of the Trustees before dinner. I was at the end of the top table next to Lady Cowan (whose husband is the Governor General) who was really very nice, easy and human.

Sir Noel Foley was in the chair and made competent introductions. The GG made a charming and erudite speech (he's an academic) – quoting from Kay Clark's *Animals and Men*.

STATEMENT IN 200 WORDS by PS.

Which I was asked to submit to EXCO.

1. The concern of the WWF is the natural environment—its animals & plants and the ecological web which binds them together with climate, soil & water into those healthy ecosystems which for centuries Man has characterised by the word "Nature".

2. WWF pays particular attention to endangered species & those which have been seriously depleted by the impact of Man, & to endangered natural habitats.

3. At the same time WWF is acutely aware of the causal factors which make nature conservation so necessary and urgent — the problems of human population increase, of high Technology agriculture, of industrialisation and urbanisation, of pollution, of misuse & waste of resources and energy, of famine and poverty.

4. If solutions to these problems can be found, WWF's aims will be more easily achieved, for it is clear that the conservation of nature cannot be dealt with in isolation from the human condition.

5. But in view of the limited funds at present available, WWF's priority projects are mainly, though not exclusively, directed Towards wildlife—defined as animals and plants and their wild habitats, and towards the promotion of public awareness of the immediate dangers that threaten nature and the steps necessary to avert them.

The objectives of the World
Wildlife Fund, requested by its
Executive Council in 1979

Quote by P.S.

" What we have done to the great whales in the sacred name of commerce is ~~a gross debasement~~ of human ~~dignity~~ an affront to *a debasement of human values* & sensibility. These magnificent animals — almost certainly the largest that have ever existed on earth, and now recognised as the possessors of outstanding intelligence — have been brought to the brink of extinction by killing methods of appalling cruelty.

I have personally witnessed and timed the death throes of a Minke whale — the smallest of the baleen whales — which was still active 4½ minutes after being hit by an explosive harpoon, *in its rear end* and was probably still alive 8 minutes after being struck. In the case of larger whales the time may be 30 minutes or even more.

Consider your reaction if you watched someone go into a field & harpoon a cow in the rump, which then took that long to die.

In the light of present knowledge of these intelligent mammals, no civilised person can contemplate the whaling industry without revulsion and shame at the insensitivity of ~~the~~ our own species. "

On my way to Australia I wrote into my diary a paraphrase of a press statement I had made before a recent meeting of the International Whaling Commission.

My speech was a bit too long and not very smooth but it seemed to be received quite well. I wish I were a more polished and fluent speaker. I get plenty of practice these days but don't seem to get much better at it and continue to dread having to do it. Maybe at the end of this ten day period I shall have become a bit more fluent and persuasive.

THURSDAY 19 APRIL

To Melbourne by 0800 flight with Vin Serventy, David Mitchell and Adrian Stark.

Then to the Sir Colin McKenzie Sanctuary at Healesville in the very plush Bentley belonging to Don Malcomson (ICI) who is a Nature Trustee.

A big (too long) lunch with the Director, Graeme George. The Director of Melbourne Zoo, Jim Sullivan, was also there. After lunch there was all too little time to see the Platypuses (and handle one), a Leadbeater's Possum (greatly endangered according to Vin). Healesville is quite well done. The Noctarium is excellent. Afterwards we motored over to Hurstbridge where Clifton Pugh* lives (his house is called 'Dunmoochin'). He was in good form, and we saw his Wombat which bit my shoes, his Emu which sat down, as on eggs, to be stroked, and his pix, many erotic.

Back to Melbourne for dinner at the Melbourne Club – Malcolmson in the chair. Two tables – places changed at the end. Food excellent. Short speech quite successful.

Rather a bad night.

FRIDAY 20 APRIL

Melbourne. 0900. Radio interview with Elizabeth Bond followed by 20 minutes of 'phone-in questions.

1100. Meeting with Victorian Premier – Rupert Hamer (who is thought unlikely to win the forthcoming election). Issues we talked about were the Murray river and the Alpine Park (which should be a joint operation between the Federal Government and Victoria and New South Wales).

Botanic Gardens for pix of Black Swans and me for press.

1230. Institute of Directors' lunch at Hilton Hotel. Speech more or less OK.

1415. Press Conference – with TV interview.

1600. To Melbourne Zoo for TV with pelicans and evening walk round zoo, which is rather good.

1800. Meeting with Victorian Conservationists, followed by long 'bun-fight' (sandwiches).

Two days of excellent bird watching (I counted 58 species) were

---

* Distinguished Australian painter who much later painted an official portrait of me for the University of Birmingham, in my robes as Chancellor.

10 Freckled Ducks at Serendip
Stictonetta naevosa

were welcome respite: first at Serendip Farm outside Melbourne then in the countryside north of Adelaide. After more interviews, I was on my way again to Perth.

WEDNESDAY 25 APRIL

Perth. With Dom Serventy [from CSIRO] and Vin and Barry Cocks to Pelican Point in the Swan River Estuary. There is a raised viewing point with a plaque commemorating Prince Philip's visit in 1963 (during the Commonwealth Games in Perth) when he persuaded the then responsible Minister to move the proposed town at Two People Bay near Mount Gardner so as to save the area for the Noisy Scrub Bird.

From the Look Out we could overlook a small pond with stilts. Grey Teal and two Grey Plover. Beyond were Australian Pelicans and Caspian Terns.

I had a TV interview there – then we walked along the sandy shore behind the pond and along the beach. Only the Grey Teal and the Pelicans remained undisturbed by us – the teal swimming quietly round the far side of the pond – about eight of them.

On to Herdsman Lake – a swamp of about 1,000 acres in the city

<u>Mon. 23.</u> Adelaide.
  2 Radio prog. Meeting with Premier of S.A.
  Businessman's lunch.   Des Corcoran (Lab)
  2 TVs.   Rob Dempsey
  Meeting with Cons Groups.   (Young)

---

p.m. *Flew to Perth.*
11.30 pm. local (0100 our time)
Meeting with the Prime Minister Malcolm Fraser.
                    at the Sheraton Hotel, Perth.

1. How it has gone. ✓ Speeches TV. Radio. Mtgs
                        Trustees. Dirs. Cons Groups.

2. Whales. Leadership ✓
            Implementation of Frost Recommendat⁰ⁿˢ

3. Conservationists worried about decreased
                                    support.

4. ~~Master~~ Membership Drive.

5. R.D.B's for Australia.

6. Regional Initiatives. PNG
                    Pacific Is.

        Commonwealth Regional Conference
        Marine Cons, Turtles, Dugongs,
        Crocodiles etc.

White-winged Wren
Malurus leucopterus

limits. Very little open water – rather like Martin Mere. It *could* be made into a wild area Wildfowl Trust operation. We did a TV interview overlooking it but sadly didn't talk about its potentialities for such development.

Then on to the CSIRO station in Helena Valley to meet Stephen Davies – tall, greying, with an English wife, who has studied doves at the Madingley Animal Behaviour Department [of Cambridge University]; we met him in 1956 at the Humpty Doo rice station near Darwin when we were filming for *Faraway Look*. He took me round his research station where there are Noisy Scrub Birds, one male and three females, some bowerbirds, many cockatoos, Emus, doves etc. Also silvereyes.

In the evening I caught a plane to Sydney.

THURSDAY 26 APRIL
The last lap in my journey: a day trip to Brisbane and back to Sydney in the evening.

FRIDAY 27 APRIL
Rather a good night's rest in the Menzies Hotel, Sydney. Breakfasted off the fruit in my room.

Vin telephoned with suggestions for my lunch-time speech to the South Pacific National Parks Conference.

Soames Summerhays [diving companion on Lindblad cruises] telephoned saying he was not coming to Pulau Redang with Ron and Val Taylor as he couldn't afford it. The ticket was A$600. I suggested I would pay his fare from a grant source, but at first he wouldn't hear of it. However I explained that I regarded his presence as *important*, because I wanted to discuss his new techniques for assessing the health and wellbeing or otherwise of coral reefs, and hopefully try them out 'on the coral'. I think he was pretty pleased to be coming and so was Val whom I spoke to next and who will bring sheets for us! She and Ron have of course been to the place already. I sensed that she was pleased Soames could now be part of the party.

We went down to the Opera House where the National Parks conference is being held. I was received by Graham Saunders of National Parks and Wildlife Queensland who told me what people had been talking about and made suggestions for my speech. Don Johnstone (Parks NSW) took me up to the coffee break where I met several state Ministers (though Paul Landa, who invited me, was not there).

Back in the conference room – which was where we had the Trustees' dinner with the Governor General on the day of my arrival in Australia – I was given a place at the table to listen to Ray Dasmann summing up. As usual Ray was authoritative, gentle and very eloquent. He is something of a pessimist. The conference seemed to have been as inconclusive as most such conferences seem to be, but no doubt it is useful for the people involved to get to know each others' faces.

At the end of the session we moved to lunch tables on a kind of indoor terrace where many were sitting already eating, and there was nothing but orange to drink. There were three State Ministers at my table and one Fijian.

The audience, when I came to speak, stretched away on either hand with none in front, but if you turned to either side you were 'off-mike' and inaudible. My piece was more or less a lead balloon.

I had to go off to the plane before the end of the lunch. Then to Singapore and on to Kuala Lumpur where I was met and driven to Carcosa – the British High Commission.

SATURDAY 28 APRIL

Having arrived at near midnight I didn't meet the Hawleys till breakfast.

In the late morning I went into town to buy some paper and card to paint and draw on, so as to provide some 'art work' for auction at the WWF Turtle Ball on 12 May.

Back in time for a swim with the Hawleys before lunch beside the pool. Yellow-vented Bulbuls, Magpie Robins, sunbirds and a kingfisher were all in evidence during lunch.

I spent the afternoon preparing my speech notes for the Annual Dinner and Ball of the Royal Society of St George to be attended by all the English expatriates in Malaysia. Phil was due to arrive from London and the plane was delayed from 1700 to 1900, so we heard. The chances of getting her off the plane and through the customs in time to reach the ball on time (which was important because of Malaysian royalty due to attend) seemed slender.

However later news indicated that the plane had caught up some time and would be coming in at 1815. The thought that I might not be at the airport to meet my darling had quite clouded my afternoon so the later news was a great relief. The plane came in only a few minutes after 1815. But many planes were landing around that time so we feared it would be some time before we could get started back to Carcosa. From the balcony we watched her come out of the plane and be met by one of the MAS girls. She had her Hong Kong sun hat with her. Later, from a gallery overlooking the baggage carousel, I caught her attention with our contact whistle. She turned out to be in very good form in spite of the long journey.

When we reached Carcosa we had just 20 minutes to dress in DJ and long dress before we had to leave with Sir Donald and Lady Hawley in the Daimler.

It was a great (and much admired) decision of Phil's to come to the dinner which she began to regret later.

The young Prince – son of the Sultan of Selangor, was very pleasant and easy – and had a charming and rather beautiful wife. He was in a white DJ and she in 'shocking pink'. The decor of the room was very colourful and clearly a great deal of trouble had been taken by all concerned. The President of the Society – Mike Ridding – made a very amusing speech, which poked fun at the Scots, the Welsh and the Irish. This set me a difficult task, but eventually they laughed so much that my speech lasted 21 minutes instead of the allotted 10, but they called for more, so it was their fault!

The dancing went on and on, and until the Royals left we could not get away. At 0145 they went and we could be taken back to Carcosa in the Daimler, leaving the Hawleys dancing for another couple of hours.

MONDAY 30 APRIL

Flew to Kuala Trengganu. About 1400 boarded *Four Friends* bound for Pulau Redang for the three-and-a-half hour journey – passing the refugee island Bidong on which 46,000 Vietnamese have been landed.

Four Friends is a very fine boat which has been lent us to make an underwater film, of which I am to be the *compère*, for WWF Malaysia. We arrived at the island in the late afternoon. We are all (about 25) to sleep in an empty clove warehouse. Apart from us this settlement is totally uninhabited although there is a village on the other side of the island which is still occupied by local people.

MONDAY 30 APRIL TO MONDAY 7 MAY

Our memorable sojourn on Pulau Redang.

Our warehouse consisted of a kitchen at ground floor level with

Peter Scott.
1979

Blue-throated
    Bee-eater
Merops viridis

Genting Highlands
  Near Kuala Lumpur
29.4.79.

Peter, Soames Summerhays and Ken Scriven – and the warehouse, Pulau Redang

a raised part with two bedrooms, a lobby and a large open verandah with a roof over it.

We had the front bedroom, Ron and Val Taylor the other one, and about 20 people, including Peter Beaumont and 10-year-old son Simon, Ken Scriven, Soames Summerhays, and an assortment of film-makers and biologists all slept in the covered verandah.

During the 9 days and 8 nights not a cross word was heard. It was a lovely time.

The days were a potpourri of filming, sound recording, SCUBA diving and snorkelling – with an evening warm bath in the fresh water lagoon behind the beach, which had at least three, maybe four species of fish in it. Tiny Mouse Deer came most evenings to drink in the lagoon but they were very shy and it was difficult to get a good look at them.

Our provisions included a number of live chickens which were kept in quite large open meshed baskets. One night a large monitor lizard made a hole in one of the baskets, climbed in and killed and ate one of the chickens. It then tried to get out through a hole in the other side of the basket. Having got its head out its legs became stuck and in the morning it was still there, immobilized. We extricated it and took it to the beach for some photographs. When put down on the sand it remained immobile as if in a trance. Phil (five foot four inches tall) lay down beside it to give scale, and it was several inches longer than her. We stood back and waited for it to move, expecting it to run up the beach into the thick bushes, but

Mouse Deer or Chevrotain
Tragulus javanicus
    About a foot high at the shoulder.

when it suddenly decided to run, it turned and ran straight into the sea. Concerned that it might be disorientated I went into the water, caught it and laid it on the beach again. Several of us were between it and the waves, but when it decided to run, it went directly past us and into the sea a second time. Only then did we realize that it clearly felt safer in the sea.

The birds consisted of White-breasted Sea Eagles, Black-naped Terns, Shamas and a prinia. Phil saw a Common Sandpiper.

Underwater the genetic diversity was much greater. We recorded 191 species of fishes.

Valerie Taylor took Phil diving with SCUBA which went very smoothly. The first dive was in shallow water and she learnt to clear her mask and take it off.

Two days later she dived again and I dived with her for the first time. This was in about 20 feet over on the coral of the island opposite the clove warehouse. Phil stayed down for about 25 minutes, but had trouble with a too-large mouthpiece.

On the following day she had her third SCUBA dive in the same general area but in about 30 feet of water. This time she was much more comfortable except for one moment when she had trouble equalizing. I beckoned her down to look under a coral head where a *Chaetodon adiergastos* juvenile was swimming upside down in a cave. I tugged her down at a time when she had not equalized and should have been allowed to go up a little to clear her ears. However it apparently wasn't too disastrous.

The third dive was much the most successful and enjoyable for her, she said. After 30 minutes we all went up. Simon (who had also been learning SCUBA from Valerie), Soames and Ron were all diving with us. We took Phil back to the shore and went out again to look at *Amphiprion polymnus* [a clown fish] which Soames had discovered out on the sand and which Ron and Val wanted to photograph and film – and which I badly wanted to see.

Meanwhile Soames and Ron found a couple of anemones. In the first the clown fish retired inside the anemone and when Ron

Abudefduf notatus

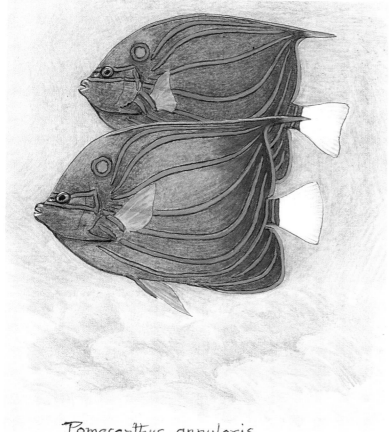

Pomacanthus annularis
The Blue-ringed Angelfish.

Monitor Lizard caught in chicken basket, and immobilized by it.

touched it the anemone went down into the sand leaving scarcely a trace of the spot. Ron came to take me to another anemone which Soames had found. He led me down – but too fast for my ears. But as usual Val stayed close to me. And eventually we came to *A. polymnus.*

It was a striking black and white fish with orange-yellow pectoral fins and lips. The adult pair was quite large and there were 4 or 5 young fish which were dull orange and white. The anemone was pale pinkish and quite unlike any other anemone I have ever seen. Its structure was like a huge wide open water lily with irregular tongue-shaped petals studded with tiny stubby tentacles.

Outside the tentacles, on the sand, was a round red patch, almost precisely circular and consisting of a carpet of eggs about $3\frac{1}{2}''$ in diameter.

After we had watched the parents fanning the eggs and being aggressive to the young fish, Ron and Valerie decided to see what would happen if *we* appeared to become aggressive to the fish. This produced an astonishing chain of events. The small fish went to the centre of the tentacles and began to burrow into the tentacles' base. The anemone began to fold up and go down into the sand. Then the two adult fish began to burrow at the centre and the last of the tentacles folded over them. Within seconds the whole anemone, with all the fish inside, had disappeared under the sand and the movement of sand at the surface had been enough to cover the scarlet egg-mass so that nothing whatever showed to distinguish that particular part of the sea bed.

I went off to find another anemone, failed to find it, and eventually turned back to see whether the original anemone had re-emerged. Three or four minutes may have elapsed, but to my astonishment all was back to normal and the eggs were being fanned by the parent fish again.

FRIDAY 11 MAY

Kuala Lumpur. Meeting with Datu Hussein Onn, Prime Minister of Malaysia. He was quite astonishingly knowledgeable about conservation matters. We talked about the New National Parks Act – about the proposed sanctuaries in Sabah and Sarawak – about the disappearing tropical rain forest and about the prospect of Marine Parks in Malaysia. We also talked of wildlife tourism possibilities.

SATURDAY 12 MAY

1000 meeting with Ong Kee Hui (pronounced Ong Ki *Wi*), Minister of Science, Technology and the Environment. He is a charming, witty little Chinese with a very good understanding of the major conservation issues, although the Federal Government has very little power over the States – to whom all the land belongs.

Endau Rompin – the forest area where logging is still taking place in a Reserve for Rhinos etc – is partly in Johore, but mostly in

Family of Clown Fish
Amphiprion polymnus

on a sandy bottom at c. 35 feet,
with scarlet egg mass & 3 juveniles,
perhaps of a previous brood from
the same parents.

Pahang. Johore has put a stop to the illegal logging. But Pahang has not done so. The Ruler (Sultan) has business interests in timber and the situation has been further complicated by his recent election as 'King' of Malaysia for a 5-year period.

The possibility of the Federal Government withholding financial aid to states which do not practise conservation is considered still to be rather remote.

We talked of Malaysia's rain forest which is disappearing at a rate of two acres a minute day and night. If this continues no low-land rain forest will be left by 1990 – and lowland forests are the richest in species and so harbour the highest genetic diversity of wildlife.

In the evening we went to WWF's 'Turtle Ball' at the Kuala Lumpur Hilton – a fund raising occasion. I had made a few drawings for the auction – mostly of coral fish, but some birds too. When they had all gone I was prevailed upon to do some sketches on the spot and these too were auctioned for ridiculously high figures. In the end the Ball made quite a surprising amount of money. Altogether my eight drawings brought in Malaysian $8,600 (about £2,000).

SUNDAY 13 MAY
Exactly one month after leaving England Phil and I flew out of Kuala Lumpur homeward bound.

CHAPTER 5

China Joins the World Wildlife Fund

DIARY 35 1979

MONDAY 17 SEPTEMBER 1979

Off to China. The usual pre-departure rush much intensified by my departure a week earlier for a tour of Wildfowl centres and then Species Survival Commission meetings in Cambridge. They were hard-working days being in the chair for the full commission meetings – about 70 people plus some Cambridge dons invited to see how IUCN works.

We are establishing a Species Conservation Monitoring Unit in a building on the University Farm where the Red Data Books [of endangered species] will be coordinated and computerized. SSC's 30th birthday coincided with my 70th so on the 11th (3 days ahead of time) they gave a party for me. Richard Fitter made the main speech. It was nice to have old Leofric Boyle, who was Chairman of SSC before me, making a reminiscent speech about the early days of the Commission.

At the end of the meetings I drove to London for World Wildlife Fund Executive Council meetings. In the evening was a dinner meeting of the Nominations Committee of WWF International with Anton Rupert in the chair at Grosvenor House.

Next day [12th September] the Executive Council met at Rothman's headquarters in Hill Street with lunch in the building and a birthday presentation to me – a book of birds of prey stuffed with envelopes containing cheques for the Wildfowl Trust which I had let drop would be the most acceptable birthday presents.

I was able to get to Paddington to meet Phil off the train and, while I stood waiting, I opened the envelopes. With two more contributions at the Athenaeum dinner for my birthday, the total was £5,710 for the Trust, plus books and other nice presents. I was very pleased that so many of my old friends came. The speeches by John London, Prince Bernhard (who had flown over specially for it), Gerry Norman, David Attenborough, Luc Hoffmann and Max Nicholson, Guy Mountfort, Richard Fitter and Russ Train were all heart-warming.

Next morning (13th) I drove Phil and Joan Kleinwort down to Slimbridge, and had almost immediately to leave again to go back up to Painswick and Paradise for the opening ceremony of 'Open Day' at Paradise House Training College for Young People in need

131

of Special Care. Friedrich and Eli Roder do a marvellous job with the autistic young people. It is a remarkable place with an atmosphere of happiness. The garden is 'environmentally friendly' – compost and all that. It is very well done, and a beautiful place (it was a beautiful day too) and I liked Friedrich and Eli. Perhaps I *should* pay more attention to the misfortunate.

Back home in the late afternoon I had time to walk round the grounds and watched the newly fledged Brown Violet-eared Hummingbird – still with a very stumpy tail – learning to catch *Drosophila* in our Tropical House. Quiet dinner with Joan Kleinwort, Tim, Dafila and Falcon. Phil had cooked some lovely trout. It was peaceful and delightful.

Friday 14th was my 70th birthday – a quiet day at home with the family.

On Sunday there was a second birthday party, this time for Wildfowl Trust staff celebration. There was a big lunch in the Trust's Hayward Foyer. I attended in a big brown wig which caused some merriment. My very old friend Rick Pilcher (in excellent form)

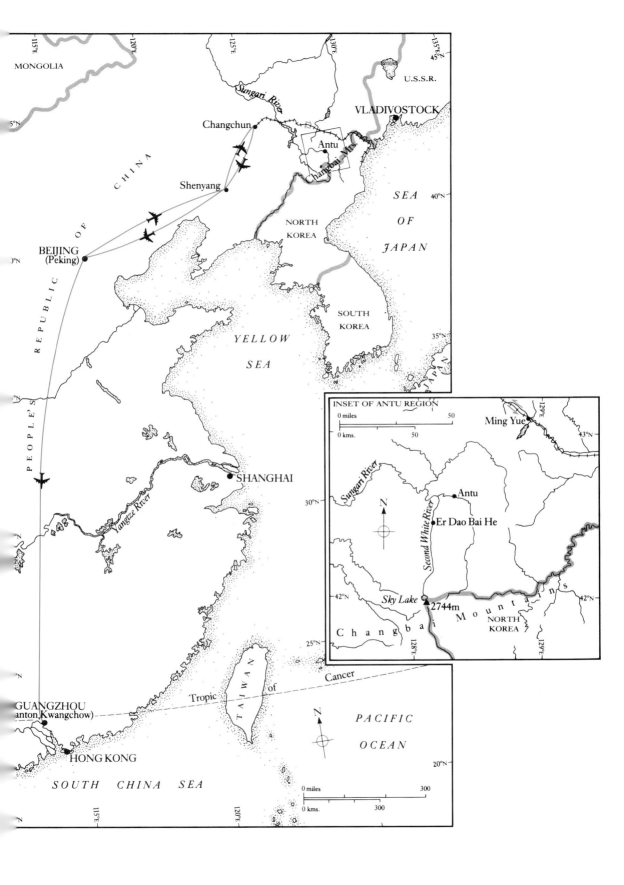

MONGOLIA

Sungari River

U.S.S.R.

VLADIVOSTOCK

Changchun

Antu

Shenyang

Changbai Mts.

C H I N A

SEA

OF

JAPAN

NORTH
KOREA

40°N

BEIJING
(Peking)

SOUTH
KOREA

35°N

R E P U B L I C   O F

YELLOW

SEA

P E O P L E ' S

SHANGHAI

30°N

Yangtze River

INSET OF ANTU REGION

0 miles   50

0 kms.   50

Ming Yue

43°N

Sungari River

Antu

Er Dao Bai He

N

Second White River

30°N

42°N

Sky Lake

2744m

M o u n t a i n s

42°N

C h a n g b a i

NORTH
KOREA

25°N

128°E

129°E

GUANGZHOU
anton,Kwangchow)

Tropic   of   Cancer

N

PACIFIC

OCEAN

T A I W A N

HONG KONG

20°N

SOUTH   CHINA   SEA

0 miles   300

0 kms.   300

115°E

120°E

125°E

130°E

135°E

45°N

115°E

120°E

completely failed to recognize me. It was especially nice that Master
(the Duke of Beaufort – who is a Trustee of the Wildfowl Trust)
should have come, and Luc Hoffmann and Max Nicholson. David
Brassey, as Chairman of the Trust Council, made the introductory
speech, then Keith [Shackleton] who was extremely funny. I had
to reply but kept off the set-piece funnies. In the evening I had to
alter a picture and write a number of thank-you letters, and sign a
lot of Special Appeal letters.

So next day away to the airport with Mike Garside reading papers
to me and taking dictated replies for the first half of the journey and
then, when he took the wheel, signing letters etc on the motorway
and in the car park, and eventually finishing them all after checking
in at the airport. Finally a last telephone call to Phil about a lawsuit
arising from the recent publication of a tiresome book about my
father. Certainly Phil will handle it very well. She is so wise and
sensible, and I am *so* lucky.

My plane – a Boeing 727 – bound for Belgrade, landed first at
Zagreb where I was handed a card from Charles de Haes [Director
General of the World Wildlife Fund] saying he'd be coming in on
the next flight in time for us to go on together – and so he did. At
once he set about charming the 'welcome hostess' which served us
in good stead.

To meet us in Peking were Lee Talbot [then Conservation
Director of WWF], David Mitchell [then PR Director for WWF Inter-
national], and Nancy Nash [journalist and wildlife enthusiast]
standing on a balcony above our entry door with a huge green WWF
Panda banner hanging over the balustrade. We were swept through
passport control and customs in no time and were soon on the long
road to the city. It was a warm evening.

Nancy Nash from Hong Kong has organized the whole visit and
persuaded the government of the People's Republic of China to
invite us. I had met her once in Morges in Charles's flat when I had
misidentified her and, thinking I had met her before, embraced her
warmly! Her success in getting the mission invited has been quite
remarkable. She speaks some Chinese and understands it fairly well.
Everyone is amazed that she was able to fix the invitation which is
the first ever to a non-governmental conservation organization.

WEDNESDAY 19 SEPTEMBER

0900 dark suits for a formal visit to the Environmental Protection
Office (EPO) who are our hosts. The Director is a rather frightening
man, Mr Li Chaobo (pronounced not so differently from Lee
Talbot!). The EPO is a body which is slightly *above* most of the
Government Ministries and Departments, having the last word on
pollution etc.

The meeting began with a formal opening followed by the amazing
announcement that the PRC had agreed to adhere immediately to
the CITES convention and to join IUCN forthwith. Two of our major

吳　Wu
作　Tso
人　Ren

A famous painter.

Photo given to me
by Prof Cheng Tso-Hsin
at the banquet
on 19.9.79
in Peking.

objectives already in the bag without any effort on our part. They also announced that a new Environmental Law had been passed which, among other things, requires an Environmental Impact Statement before any land development can go ahead. The law had been passed on my 70th birthday, which I told them (somewhat rashly). From then on they have constantly referred to my great age – how fit I am etc etc. (They probably knew this from my passport anyway.)

Mr Li left before we got down to the detail. We were told that it was *most* unusual to have the Director and two Vice-Directors present at the start of the meeting.

Altogether they have shown great cordiality. They evidently mean business in the conservation field. The day ended with a banquet hosted by the EPO.

> There followed two days of meetings and visits to the Museum of Natural History and the Peking Zoo, ending with a memorable banquet at the Beihai 'Palace' at which we were the hosts.

SATURDAY 22 SEPTEMBER

Morning from 0730–1030 spent on planning the press conference for tomorrow evening. The 1700 arrangement had to be abandoned because of a planned large scale 'demo' by people who suffered injustice under the 'Gang of Four' and are seeking reinstatement.

Then we were off in the cars – first to pay the bill for last night's party at the Beihai Palace – with its lake covered with boats.

On to the Summer Palace for lunch. The visit was short but very pleasant. We walked along the shore of the lake, passing along the covered way which has been newly painted. It seemed to me many of the paintings were newly designed. We saw two painters actually at work, and one was painting an aquatic scene apparently without copying it from anything.

In the two cars driven by our aggressive and rather disagreeable drivers, who had lunch with us, we went to the Great Wall.

SUNDAY 23 SEPTEMBER

Press Conference 1900. I announced the signing of the Conservation Agreement between the PRC and the World Wildlife Fund. Charles announced that the PRC had agreed to join IUCN and adhere to CITES. Lee talked about the 'World Conservation Strategy'* and answered questions with consummate skill.

There were one or two needling questions from Western journalists. 'Would the PRC *really* join CITES or just talk about it?'; 'Would they *really* stop the import of rhino horn?'; 'Would they *really* control the importation of ivory?' etc. Also questions about the total number of Wild Pandas. We have been given estimates from '350–400' up to '1,000'. Apparently there had recently been a report that only 60 were left after the bamboo disease of 2 years

---

* See page 108 also for a description of the strategy.

1430. 20.9.79. Translations by Mr Yuan.

Glad to welcome Mr Zhang Shu-Zhong,

Mr Qin Tsien~~Hta~~ Hua, Mr Wang ~~Man-Hu~~ Meng-Hu, Mr Chao Ching-Lou etc.

Chief Wildlife Dept. of
Min. of Forestry & Nature
          Conservation.

1st Question from Mr ~~Kin~~ Chin Tsien Ming
    "What is the W.C.S.?"
PS on meaning of word 'Strategy'-
Lee T. on what WCS is and hopes to do.
   3 Major Goals.
      ① To maintain 'life support systems.' (Ecological processes)
            e.g. Global bio-geo-chemical cycles. Nitrogen) Cycles
                  Water flow   Carbon)
                                                  Oxygen

      ② To maintain 'genetic diversity'
            genetic material in all living things.
               a. for direct use by man e.g. China uses 4,000 plants
                     food, medicine etc.   for medecine.
               b. biological values, biological control.
               c. Role of spp in the breeding stocks of domestics. etc.
                                    life support system.
               Values to man only 1% known. Other 99%
                  probably have values as yet unknown.
            40% of prescriptions in US are based on wild plants or
      ③ To assure that where species or ecosystems   wild animals
          are being used, the use is sustainable.
            e.g. forests, grasslands, fisheries etc -
         Climbing human pop. against overall reduction
            of capacity of earth to sustain such a pop.

Conservation in the past has been regarded as a thing apart.
Different Ministries want to do their thing & set conservation
to one side. Now W.C.S.
Framework for action. National Action Plans.
                        International Action.
New Thrust Cons + Devt are essential one to another

21.9.79.
  PEKING ZOO **56** ha.

Pandas first kept in 1955.
 Difficult to keep them.
Academy of Sciences studied them in the wild.
  2600 m. a.s.l. Rather warm & very wet.
              Lots of Bamboo.
  Food in captivity is a problem –
  First cub born in 1963
    from then 11 born but only 8 survived
              Sometimes twins.
Reproduction rate not high in wild.
    Problems with reproduction because food &
      climate are different in captivity.
    When only a pair difficulty of timing when on heat.
A.I. began in 1978 — one success — Yuan Zhin
                                      (Jin).
As near to natural conditions needed in captivity.
More study needed.... ongoing studies at present.
More needed on rythm of life –
Want other zoos to have success –

  Fur not v. thick. Temp. controlled by moving
up & down mountains & from sunny to shady side.
Forest v. dense — protective colouring not needed –
Pandas rest in tops of trees.
 Life span 20 – 30 yrs.
 Longest in Peking Zoo 27 yrs.
  More than 20 in other zoos – 4 in Peking.

Estimated total number of wild Giant Pandas :
    between 400 and 1,000.
Found only in mountainous bamboo forests of Szechuan, Kansu & Chensi.

ago. But it seems that that figure was for only one of the three provinces in which they occur.

After it Charles, Lee, Nancy and I went by taxi to the post office – Nancy to telex the agreed text of the press release and the rest of us, armed with beer, to give her moral support. It took about two hours to get the typing done and get it fed into the machine transmitting it to the headquarters of WWF in Switzerland.

PRESS RELEASE ISSUED EX PEKING 23 SEPTEMBER.

WWF signs agreement with China. WWF announced at a press conference in Beijing today that it has reached an agreement for cooperation in conservation with the People's Republic of China.

The agreement, which was signed before the conference, calls for the immediate establishment of a WWF China committee of six members – three from WWF International and three from the recently formed Association for Environmental Sciences of the PRC.

The WWF China committee will coordinate links between conservation organizations and authorities in China and WWF worldwide contacts. It will initiate high priority projects in China and will coordinate action for their implementation.

The agreement was signed today by the Vice-Director of the Environment Protection Office of the State Council, Mr Qu Geping, and the Chairman of WWF International Sir Peter Scott, who described it as a 'truly historic occasion for world conservation'.

Sir Peter is leading a five-member WWF delegation to China – the first non-governmental conservation organization ever to receive an official invitation from the Chinese government.

Under new environmental laws passed in Beijing during the WWF delegation visit, environmental impact assessment studies are now a compulsory component of all future development planning in China.

WWF's Swiss-based Director Mr Charles de Haes, who is also part of the WWF delegation, announced two other key conservation decisions by the Chinese government: under the first, China has agreed to become a state member of IUCN, the major scientific arm of world conservation, with over 50 sovereign state members included in its total membership of 450 state, government agencies and non-governmental organizations from over 100 nations. China has agreed immediately to accede to CITES. This move is of particular significance since China is one of the major trading nations in wild plants and animal products.

Mr de Haes said, 'The fact that China has made these commitments and is about to assume a leadership role in conservation may well be considered the most significant single development in conservation since the UN conference on the human environment held in Stockholm in 1972.

'China, with almost a quarter of the world's population, is facing up to problems which are of crucial importance to man everywhere in his continuing efforts to achieve a harmonious balance with nature.

'This is going to be a two-way street with a full and continuing exchange of information. IUCN/WWF have developed conservation techniques through their work in many countries which are of interest here, and by the same token, we have a great deal to learn from the successful conservation measures which have been developed in the PRC,' he added.

WWF Director of Conservation and Species, Dr Lee Talbot, said, 'China has recorded more than 2,100 species of vertebrate animals (mammals, birds, reptiles, amphibians and fishes). Some of these species are in danger and insufficient data exists on which to base a sound campaign to bring them back from the brink of extinction. We have a number of projects now under discussion in this category and we hope to be able to make an announcement on the first ever international projects in China within a matter of weeks as a first step in implementing the agreement we have just signed.'

Dr Talbot, who addressed the Chinese Academy of Sciences in Beijing on Monday on latest developments in international conservation, said the WWF delegation had expressed the hope that the Chinese government would play a major role in implementing the World Conservation Strategy now being developed by IUCN under the joint sponsorship of WWF and UNEP:

'The strategy which is now in final draft form seeks to bridge the past gulf between conservation and development and to show for the 1980s that conservation and development must work as one. It is a philosophy which we understand is now shared by the government of the PRC.'

In addition to EPO, the WWF delegation has had wide-ranging and productive talks with other governmental and scientific authorities, including the Minister of Forestry and the Chinese Academy of Sciences through its Institutes of Zoology and Botany and the Museum of Natural History and Beijing Zoo.

WWF, with headquarters in Switzerland and national organizations in 27 countries, is the leading international organization raising and disbursing funds for conservation.

China is the only home of the Giant Panda, the animal adopted as the WWF symbol at the time of its founding in 1961. Giant Pandas are found in the wild only in the mountainous bamboo forests of Sichuan, Gansu, and Shaanxi provinces in the interior of China.

MONDAY 24 SEPTEMBER

0700 departure from the Peking Hotel for the Government-organized excursion to 'the north-east' – formerly Manchuria. The party includes the five of us on the delegation, our interpreter Mr Yuan and Mr Cho (thought to be or have been a policeman). Also on the Chinese side were Mr Gao and Mr Zhou Xianrong from EPO, Qin Qianhua from Forestry, and Mr Sun Chang Jang (naturalist).

The first leg was 1½ hours to Shenyang in Liaoning Province. The airport hall had six big portraits – ahead Chairman Mao and Chairman Hua, on the left Marx and Engels, on the right Lenin and Stalin.

Next stop Changchun at 1140. There we were met by a large group of local dignitaries headed by Mr Chen who is Deputy Director of EPO in Changchun – which is a city of 1.2 million inhabitants.

We were driven to the VIP guest house and given a large lunch with many toasts in *mao tai* each demanding a 'bottoms up' response. The food was about the best we have had in China. After lunch a visit to the top floor of a department store which was a Friendship Store where I bought some small things as presents. Then the 'Zoo'.

Changchun Zoo is very crumby indeed though it has a nice setting in a public park. The cages for a tiger, a leopard, a bear, wolves etc were small, old and dilapidated. An aviary 16 metres by 6 metres and 8 metres high was packed with 36 large water birds

Tetrastes bonasia
Hazel Grouse.
Spruce Hen

from a pelican to a Herring Gull and included 10 *Grus japonensis* [Manchurian Crane], one *G. leucogeranus* [Siberian Crane] and two *Ciconia boyciana* [Eastern White Stork]. 13 specimens of endangered species in a sadly small place, though they looked reasonably healthy. The single Bewick Swan's bill was unhealthily whitish, but the Whooper's was quite yellow. In another aviary were 3 Brown-eared Pheasants (also an endangered species).

After dinner we boarded the train for the journey to Ming Yue which was formerly the county town of Antu County.

TUESDAY 25 SEPTEMBER

We arrived in the early hours before dawn on a *very* cold morning with the clouds down low, and were taken in a motorcade of Jeeps to a guest house for breakfast. After a Chinese breakfast we set off on the four hour drive to Antu. On the way we passed a huge artificial lake with lots of ducks, but the low morning sun turned them all into silhouettes, and we made a mental note to allow time for bird watching on the way back when the afternoon light would be behind us. As it was we identified 60 Chinese Spot-billed Ducks, 20 Green-winged Teal and four Mandarin Ducks.

After lunch we went on to the Changbai Mountain Reserve headquarters at 'second White River'.

Nutcracker
Nucifraga caryocatactes

Alpine Accentor
Prunella collaris.

WEDNESDAY 26 SEPTEMBER

Up into the reserve. The road led up through the deciduous forest, supposed to contain the last few Siberian Tigers (though it seems doubtful if any are left), up into the coniferous forest and finally emerged above the tree line. Changbai Shan means 'Everwhite Mountain' and eventually we reached the snow line. We came to a point where we were invited to walk a short distance up a steepish slope to a crest with a fantastic view overlooking a small lake called 'Sky Lake' or the 'Lake of Heaven' which was surrounded by rocky peaks that were largely covered with snow. On a distant ridge on the far side of the lake we could see large numbers of people on the skyline. They were North Koreans gazing into China.

We had lunch in a mountain hut, then went on to a fine waterfall, and finally to the hot springs where we bathed.

During that day we had seen the following birds: Chinese Greenfinch, Goshawk, Hazel-hen (*Tetrastes bonasia*) (?) – or Spruce Hen – Nutcracker, Blue Turtle Dove, Alpine Accentor, Golden Eagle, Brown Dipper, warbler (*Phylloscopus*), Jay and 25 Kestrel.

THURSDAY 27 SEPTEMBER

From Antu out to the station at the reserve at Er Dao Bai He or 'second White River'. Then back, after more conservation discussion, to Antu, and after lunch the four-hour drive to the railway

at Ming Yue by way of the big reservoir. It had seemed possible
that we might find Chinese Mergansers in the lake and, of course,
our Chinese hosts fervently hoped that we should, as this species
and the Brazilian Merganser are the only waterfowl species I have
never seen alive. There were many fewer ducks than before at the
top end, but the first three my eye lit upon were 3 mergansers in
grey plumage – 1 male and 2 female, or possibly an adult female
with 2 immatures. They were a long way off, and I could not be
certain that they were not Red-breasted Mergansers which also
occur in China, but knowing that this was Chinese Merganser
country there seemed every possibility that they were *Mergus
squamatus*. The only way to distinguish the two species in eclipse
or juvenile plumage is that the position of the nostril in the Red-
breasted Merganser is marginally further from the tip of the bill
than it is in the Chinese species – not the kind of detail that can be
resolved at a range of 400 yards. The birds were not big enough, by
comparison with four Wigeon which later joined them, to be
Goosanders. It was a great moment, although I shall never know
how great a part in the diagnosis was played by good manners and
my wish to please our hosts.

At the deep end of the lake, right out in the middle, was a flock
of 192 mixed ducks. One group of three looked to me like Mandarins,
but by this time they were in silhouette against the setting sun.
Certainly there were many Spotbills and many Teal or Garganey.

FRIDAY 28 SEPTEMBER

After a night in the train, breakfast, and then I gave a lecture in the
Station Hotel at Changchun starting at 0830. Audience 190. Then
some shopping, lunch, and leave-taking of our good friends.

So back to Peking on a lovely warm evening. Lee and I talked
about projects on the long drive into town and who might do the
Panda population survey.

A Chinese delegation was due at 1930. Charles and I were planning to convert his room into a meeting room. From then on all was
slapstick farce. The Chinese were due in three minutes. Charles
and I were alone to do the conversion. We brought in chairs and
small tables from neighbouring rooms – mine, Lee's etc. At the
last minute Charles decided we should move one of the beds out.
We started carrying an end each but when it came to turning the
bed sideways to get it through the door sanity prevailed. 'You'll
have to hold the mattress and pillows on,' said Charles. 'Well I
can't,' I said, 'and the whole idea is crazy.' So we decided to put the
bed along one wall. This required that the large reclining chairs be
piled on top of one another, which Charles quickly did. Then one
of the low glass-topped tables also had to be moved and was placed
by Charles on top of the top chair. Then we pushed the bed round.
At the last moment it wouldn't go by an inch. The chairs had to be
nudged out and that was it. With a monumental crash the whole

The Chinese or Scaly-sided Merganser
= Chungkwa chu Sa Yati.
Mergus squamatus.

It breeds in the Chaingbai
Mountain Reserve.
Jilin province. PRC.

The big question
Did we see them?
Certainly not looking
like the male !

Chinese Spotbill
Anas poecilorhyncha
zonorhyncha.

Chinese Spotbills

pile collapsed, and the glass top of the table shattered into a hundred pieces.

As we stood there convulsed with laughter surveying total shambles, the first of the Chinese delegation walked into the room. The first to arrive was Li Chaobo to discuss the terms of our filming in the zoo on the following morning. There was a misunderstanding about the others so that instead of coming up to our room they waited downstairs for 20 minutes without our knowing. When they finally came up Mr Jin Jianming from EPO announced '*three Chinese members of the World Wildlife Fund/China*' – an exciting start for our discussions.

SATURDAY 29 SEPTEMBER

Up early to pack before going to Peking Zoo for filming pandas. We must have movie footage for television on our successful visit, and it has to be compulsive viewing. (Yesterday we heard that the cost of filming Pandas would not be $1,000 as agreed but $2,500– $3,000. We decided to go ahead all the same.)

We had the full cooperation of the zoo authorities and began by hanging our six-foot-square green WWF flag with its large black and white Panda symbol over the wall of the enclosure. First the young male came to look at it, then the larger female. He put his paws up on the flag, then bit at the edges and jumped back when the cloth moved. She, on the other hand, came and gazed directly at the symbol in the middle – rather larger than her. It was difficult to believe that she was not aware of the two-dimensional representation as another panda. Even though she wasn't as brave as the young male she came and ate the bamboo which I held out to her and rustled to attract her attention. In the end she pulled so hard that my little finger would have been cut if I had not let go.

Later we moved to the smaller enclosure, where the AI baby – Yang Jing or Yuan Jing – also came up to the flag, but was intimidated when I inadvertently moved the flag just as he was approaching it.

The delight of the Chinese children and their lack of shyness was marvellous. Charles and I joined hands with some of them and skipped along for the benefit of the movie cameras. I think the footage should be very well worth the $3,500 we have now had to pay for the zoo fee and camera team.

In the afternoon we caught a plane to Kwangchow. We are staying at the Tungfang Hotel where Phil and I stayed last year with the Lindblad party. The room is very similar and brought back memories. I can't wait to get back to Phil.

The 'team spirit' has been very good in our delegation of five and we all get on very well under considerable pressure of engagements, events and negotiations. Lee is very competent although a bit slow in manner and therefore seeming a little pompous. He has a certain 'ego sensitivity'. David is efficient within his press expertise. Charles is more than a little disorganized and unpunctual at times but on the whole very clear-thinking and admirably decisive. His sense of humour is splendid, and one way and another we do a great deal of laughing. Nancy is sometimes a little over-enthusiastic and gushing but she is a very competent professional journalist and press photographer, and follows things through with admirable determination. She speaks some Chinese and gets on very well with them. Surprisingly they do not seem to mind her fulsomeness. She is quite thoughtful of others. A warm-hearted person full of energy in pursuit of the main objectives.

SUNDAY 30 SEPTEMBER

An hour's drive in a minibus from the Tungfang Hotel to Whampoa Harbour – down stream from Kwangchow. The road was fairly narrow and the drive correspondingly dangerous, with heavy and frequent application of the brakes, through the lush Cantonese countryside with most of the rice at the brilliant yellow-green stage. During the drive our interpreter guide questioned us on conservation and asked, 'Which country is best at it?' It set us off on a discussion about the answer and this led to questions of comparability.

Our preliminary impressions were that the USA, UK, Netherlands,

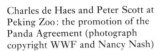

Charles de Haes and Peter Scott at Peking Zoo: the promotion of the Panda Agreement (photograph copyright WWF and Nancy Nash)

Switzerland, New Zealand and perhaps Canada were doing better in conservation than most others. In Africa Tanzania, Kenya and South Africa had been doing well until fairly recently. Now only South Africa and perhaps The Gambia. There were few countries in South America, Asia or Southern Europe doing anything at all.

How do large acreages of National Parks and reserves equate with membership of the Convention on International Trade in Endangered Species, or voting records in the International Whaling Commission? How would strong protection laws be compared with enforcement records, or with conservation's share of national budgets?

It led to the idea that we should do some work along these lines, perhaps using the kinds of techniques which have been developed by the consumer magazine *Which?* to establish 'the best buy'. The WWF might issue some sort of good housekeeping seal to needle Governments to perform better. I believe it is worth following up.

In the afternoon we arrived in Hong Kong by hydrofoil – calm weather but rather bumpy. That evening there was a party at Nancy's flat to thank the Chinese who had worked with Nancy on all the arrangements for getting us invited by the Government of the PRC.

And so home to England a few days later.

CHAPTER 6

The Far East Shuttle

DIARY 37   1980

At the beginning of 1980 a number of engagements in Japan, Hong Kong and China could be dove-tailed into a complex itinerary. The first was a conference of the International Water-fowl Research Bureau in Sapporo on the Japanese Island of Hokkaido, which our daughter Dafila was also attending as a member of the Swan Group. (Her PhD thesis had been on 'The Social Behaviour of Wintering Bewick's Swans'.) After the con-ference and its excursions, I was to represent WWF and IUCN at their ceremonies to launch the World Conservation Strategy in China and Hong Kong; national ceremonies were taking place all over the world in a single week. This involved going first to Peking to record a television interview, then to Hong Kong for another TV appearance and the actual launch, then back to Peking for the ceremony there and to meet the Deputy Prime Minister. It was a complicated shuttle programme, and what it achieved will, perhaps, remain for ever imponderable.

SATURDAY 16 FEBRUARY 1980

The night had been disturbed by a major exodus of swans from Swan Lake around midnight. At feed times under the floodlights on the previous evening there had been at least 200 Bewick's Swans on Swan Lake. By first light there were barely 75 and at first feed (0745) still only 85. By 0900 the number on Swan Lake had risen to 125. We shall not know till we get back whether the other 75 swans came in during the day or whether it was the beginning of a migration.

The last-minute pressure was heavier than ever, getting my art book *Observations of Wildlife* – boring title and not mine – finally to bed, with dedication to Phil, and acknowledgements, and with final 'whispies' [drawings in the text] to illustrate the new tower in which the book was written, the bill pattern of Lancelot, our most faithful wild Bewick's Swan back for his 17th consecutive winter, a Humpback Whale and a Lesser White-fronted Goose.

We left Heathrow on a JAL plane at 1400. On the whole the journey to Tokyo – stopping at Anchorage, with a stupendous view of Mount McKinley just before – was fairly comfortable. Phil and I had too little sleep – a bare two hours. From Tokyo we flew on to

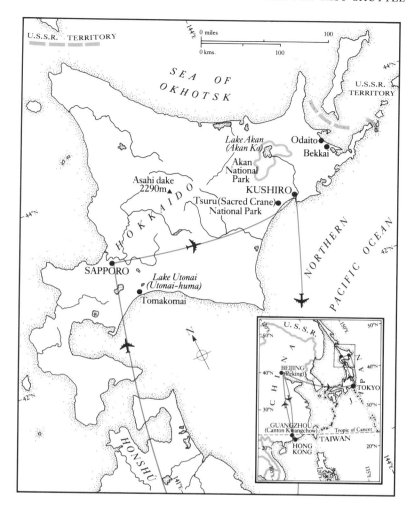

Chitose Airport in a DC8 (very cramped space). Then a bus ride
through a heavy snowstorm to the Hokkaido Koseinenkin Kaikan
– a large hotel in Sapporo – where we arrived at about 2100 for a
very late meal which was too large but very good.

So bed in room 701 was late, and not being conversant with the
heating control, we spent a rather cold night. Dafila was already in
the hotel (having had a week visiting swan resorts) and in the room
next to ours. She has a nasty cold.

MONDAY 18 FEBRUARY

Early start to meet Their Imperial Highnesses Prince and Princess
Hitachi. Assembled round a huge table were: the Governor of
Hokkaido, Mr Matsui [President of the Swan Society of Japan],
Geoffrey Matthews [Director of IWRB] and Mary ('the Swan') who

151

National Report from Japan.

Natural Monuments: <u>Nipponia nippon</u>
<u>Grus japonensis</u>
<u>Diomedea albatrus</u>
Short-Tailed Albatross.

also <u>Lutra lutra whiteleyi</u> 1979 105
(1929-2,000
1939 — 50
1959 — 22
1973 — 62)

Counts on 16th January 1979

    8,416 Whooper Swans
    2,550 Bewick's Swans
    7,830 Wild Geese.
1,287,528 Ducks

observed at 3,644 points covering 415,598 ha.
Counts regular since 1970

December 1979. 271 Grus japonensis (36 sub-adult)
in the Kushiro Marsh.   Dr H. Masatomi

Crane count. 1980, in Japan.
    4,775 Cranes : 3,962 Hooded
                     808 White-naped
                       4 Common
                       1 Sandhill.

Won, Pyong-Oh   4,000 – 5,000 Swans wintering in
                 Korea, mostly Whoopers.

were just married, Phil, me and the Prince and Princess. There were long and embarrassing pauses in the conversation. The Prince wanted to know whether Mallard were increasing in Britain. Apparently there has been, he said, a great increase of Pintails in Japan since 1960. After tea with lemon and further awkward silences it was time to move into the main meeting room.

Then the Opening Ceremony of the 26th board meeting of the IWRB. I was called on (without any warning) to give a message of greetings; Phil and Dafila seemed to think it was all right.

After the morning session (during which the only laugh was when

Geoffrey forgot the scientific name of the Coot), lunch was at 1330 and then a sudden panic developed because my lecture at the University was at 1500 and the slides were at the hotel. We were to be called for at 1430 at the conference centre but Sapporo's traffic is such that after the heavy snow fall (50 cms) of last night it was not likely we would be able to pick up the slides and arrive at the University by 1500. Nor was it. We arrived at about 1525 to find a small tiered lecture room with about 30 people scattered in a space that would hold maybe 150. Some more people came in during the lecture so that it was about half full by the end of my one hour and ten minute talk on the Wildfowl Trust and Bewick's Swans. The title had been 'The Ecology and Ethology of Wildfowl' which they had invented *faute de mieux*?

After the lecture the kind Professor rather tryingly kept us drinking tea (the car had possibly not arrived) so that we were almost late for the Noh play – only 40 minutes of it instead of 3 hours as we experienced in Tokyo at the time of the Olympic Games. This ancient traditional performance is an experience which, without specialized knowledge, we have found fascinating for the first 20 minutes.

After the Noh play, a great hustle to get to the Governor's Welcome Party with TIH Prince and Princess Hitachi. There were large ice sculptures of a pair of swans and a pair of cranes. We drank *sake* from square wooden boxes and ate raw fish and molluscs. We presented Dafila to the Prince and Princess.

TUESDAY 19 FEBRUARY

IWRB executive board meeting all day. Dafila's cold and cough giving her trouble. She felt (and looked) rather ill, but was determined to go on the excursion next morning.

WEDNESDAY 20 FEBRUARY

There was a snowstorm all the way to Lake Utonai (one and a half hours away) but it had become intermittent by the time we arrived and was not so cold. The lake is very large and was mostly frozen over with snow on the ice.

We stopped at the edge of the lake by a semi-circular arc of open water – in front of a small trickle of water from a pipe, said to be purified sewage. The radius of the unfrozen arc was about 40 yards. We were in the second bus and already there was a crowd of people from the first lining the shore. We were told that some swans had been caught in clap nets baited with crusts of bread.

About 65 swans were on the water, mostly Whoopers with a dozen or so Mutes, and walking away through the snow on the far side were another 75 Whoopers. There were no Bewick's at all. Further out on the snow sat about 30 Pintails. There were some eagles sitting out on the ice. Two of these were huge: Steller's Sea Eagles – an adult and an immature. Some distance from them and

Cygnus cygnus
Whooper Swan.

Cygnus columbianus bewickii
Bewick's Swan.

close to the swans were 4 much smaller eagles; these were White-tailed Sea Eagles. Further out on the ice were small groups of ducks which flew from time to time. Among these I saw some Chinese Spotbills and some wigeon.

Lunch with the Mayor of Tomakomai. Congratulatory speech by me, and presentation of ties.

THURSDAY 21 FEBRUARY
Swan Symposium. I had ten minutes to start it off – as Honorary Chairman. At 1000 was Dafila's paper on the Social Behaviour of Bewick's Swans. She has recovered from her cold, though not completely, and the paper went down extremely well with the audience.

Evening meeting on *Nipponia nippon* [Japanese Crested Ibis]. Only 6 birds left in Japan. One in captivity. Made strong speech that the five wild birds should now be captured.

FRIDAY 22 FEBRUARY
Second day of Swan Symposium followed by final session of the executive board of IWRB. Dafila and I did a piece with slides on 'Supplementary feeding of swans in the UK'. Ian Prestt [from the RSPB] thinks the phrase does not apply to the Trust's 'bird tables' as the birds would not die of starvation if we stopped feeding them. My part of the presentation was too long, leaving Dafila too little for hers.

154

Cheng Tso-Hsin.

Cheng on China   (and Chou (Jo) from Academy)
  at IWRB meeting.

1. Academy of Sciences. Zoology biggest institute. Ecology &
   Mainly concerned with research.   discipline Taxonomy.
2. Min of Forestry. Division on Nature Protection. Conservation Laws.

3. Environment Protection Agency. covers Natural Reserves.
   Newly established.   Imports.

4. Local + Provincial Institutes, including Research
   Institutes in Universities

Grus nigricollis   Breeding in Ching Hai Province (Tibet)
  600 seen together at one locality. (or 50 among 600 ??)
  National Reserve to be set up by Gort. at Koko Nor
Mergus squamatus. Nesting in tree holes like Mandarin Province.
                                                       Ducks.
Brown Crossoptilon: rediscovered S of formerly reported
                                                       range.

100 Natural Reserves by end of 1980.
  150 spp protected.
Three problems hopefully to be solved soon.

1. Enforcement of Game Laws.
2. Habitat Management. Conflict with industrialisation.
3. People in China are opposed to bird banding.
In answer to Geoffrey Hopes PRC may join Ramsar Convention
but cant say anything yet.

Red-crowned Cranes, Hokkaido

SATURDAY 23 FEBRUARY

We flew to Kushiro and from the airport buses took us to a lookout layby above Kushiro Moor. The marsh had been invaded by small trees due to progressive drying out. It was, of course, snow-covered but brown from dead vegetation. There is an endemic salamander which lives only in Kushiro Moor, and a number of pairs of *Grus japonensis* [Japanese Crane] breed in the marsh.

At lunch with the Mayor of Kushiro I made a congratulatory speech bringing in various points requested by the Japan Bird Society. This seems to be an important part of the whole exercise – the visitors, after thanking and congratulating, encourage the next steps forward in research and conservation. On this occasion the points were congrats on making Kushiro Moor a national monument, but don't let it dry out, on building a crane breeding facility at the Kushiro Zoo, but keep Mr Takahashi's Crane Park going as an educational and tourist attraction – the two being complementary. And congrats to Mr. T for his wonderful achievements over so many years. The Mayor of Kushiro is a youngish-looking man who was a veterinarian and seemed to think of conservation with sympathy. So let's hope my contribution will have been hoisted in.

Later we took the buses to the Crane Park which we had visited in August 1976. When we arrived they told us that there had

156

just been an earthquake (Richter Scale 4) and that all the cranes had begun to call *before* it.

There were more cranes in the park than last time [see page 13]. Most of the pinioned birds were males in separate pens and wild females had flown into each pen. The snow was quite deep, and the birds looked superb. They were being fed a small, shallow, carp-like fish.

We went up the valley to a crane feeding station where a very ambitious observatory building looked out over a snow–covered field with a wood beyond. As we approached down a very slippery side road (my synthetic rubber soles are worn quite smooth) 5 cranes flew low across in front of us. One of the five was dark-bodied, the other four white. As we went into the observatory we were told that 'the White-naped Crane had just left'. We passed through the heated observatory and down some steps on to a kind of terrace which was crowded with people. About 100 yards away were 59 Red-crowned Cranes.

From the observatory there was a different view, and while we were up there, 5 cranes came back from an open stream to which the birds had been flighting to drink. One of the five was the dark bird I had seen going there just before our arrival. It was the White-naped Crane, *Grus vipio*, which was only the second record for the Kushiro district, the previous one being last year and perhaps the same bird. It stood much more vertically than *G. japonensis*.

A man had been out to feed the cranes with maize and what looked like whitebait; they came to within four or five yards of him, but no closer.

Just before we left the sun came out, casting long evening shadows across the snow. There was a large finch in the top of a tree with white in its wing. I thought it was a grosbeak female but those who knew better than me said it was definitely a Hawfinch, *Cocothraustes cocothraustes*, though presumably not the European race *C. c. cocothraustes* (later I discovered it could only have been *C. c. japonicus*).

So on for the night to a traditional Japanese hotel (dreadfully over-heated) where we had to dress in traditional kimonos – like brown monks – and have a traditional Japanese meal with whitebait caught from a tank and cooked on the spot. The beds were made up on the floor and we watched Ainu (primitive) dances but did not partake of the communal hot spring baths (no mixed bathing).

SUNDAY 24 FEBRUARY

A long drive through the mountain forests of Akan National Park to Odaito. It is a coastal resort on the east (Pacific) coast of Hokkaido inside a huge bay protected by a sand spit, partly wooded. It is a prime wintering place for Whooper Swans. The shore was lined with chalets and where the open water came to the shore the swans were concentrated; on the ice beyond some 200–300 swans were

sleeping. We reckoned there were in all about 1,000–1,300 but were told there were over 2,000.

It being Sunday afternoon, there were crowds of people feeding the birds from packets of prepared food that looked like pop-corn. Although some were close enough to take food from the hand, I only saw one that tried to do so, and the feeder flinched. Two large sacks of oats were fed to the swans on the frozen shoreline.

Some swans had walked far up the shore almost into a car park. The local swan-banders were in the first bus and by the time we had climbed down from the second bus, the first swans had been caught just by picking them up. They caught about 5 or 6 by this method before the other swans made their way back to the water. There were one or two neck-banded birds, with green collars.

A noticeable feature of these Whoopers was the high forehead and divided crown caused by the enlarged supra-orbital glands resulting from their winter quarters being on the sea. The principal function of these glands is desalination. In most of them there was a visible central cleavage between the two glands on the crown of the head.

A Steller's Sea Eagle flew over, and Phil pointed out a Long-tailed Duck diving. There were also some Goldeneye and a number of Scaup. It was extremely cold in spite of fitful sunshine. In the early morning it had been −28°C and the strongish wind gave a high chill factor. I went back to the bus to change a film and was grateful for the respite in the warm.

After lunch at Bekkai with the Mayor – who had a sense of humour but no English (he referred to his town as 'a funny little place, tucked away in a corner of Hokkaido') – we had another three-hour bus trip via Kushiro city (Goosanders and Goldeneyes in the river as we crossed the bridge) to Kushiro Airport – where some 'Goodbyes' – and then take-off for Tokyo in another DC8. The 'tour leader' who talked to us on the bus ride into Tokyo was magnificently comical (unintentionally) in his English, his accent, his delivery and his appearance. He must have been the Japanese equivalent of Robertson Hare.

The Shiba Park Hotel where we are staying has a 'New Wing' which is the last word in hotel gadgetry including computerized lifts, so that one never had to wait more than 10 seconds. There were dimmer switches on the bedside lamps, and a tap which poured the bathwater in a clear icicle-like stream which was totally silent. But the water level in the loo-pan was a little too high for me! Ah well, no doubt it is all right for others.

Wild Whooper Swans at Odaito

MONDAY 25 FEBRUARY

Phil, Dafila and I started the day with a before-breakfast swan meeting with 14 other people; my old friend Bill Sladen was in the chair. The purpose of the meeting was for the Swan Group to discuss standardization of study techniques and terminology, and a proposed manual on the subject. (I suggested it be called *Guidelines* so as not to stifle invention and innovation.) The discussion eventually got down to detail and the perennial argument developed on the use of neck bands, and the 4-digit 'protocol' for letters and numbers on rings. [The Wildfowl Trust uses three digits which, on a given ring size, means they can be larger and therefore read at a longer range through binoculars or a telescope.] The attack on the Wildfowl Trust's 'selfishness' and 'irresponsibility' was renewed. They have a good case, but I put the opposing view of Malcolm Ogilvie, who is in charge of the Trust's ringing programme, rather as devil's advocate. Why should someone wanting, for example, long visibility of a small number of birds have to accept 4 digits (that is, readability at a more restricted range) on the off chance that it might confuse someone who recovered it somewhere on the other side of the world? My heart was not in the argument but I think half of them thought it was my point of view and not Malcolm's.

On the neck-band argument, Dafila believes it remains to be proved that they do not in any way jeopardize the birds and she is against any being used on Bewick's of known age (which she wants to work on) or any regulars at either Welney or Slimbridge. She would accept their use on a limited number of Whoopers, and perhaps a few not previously known adults (of unknown age) – but not on cygnets or yearlings until much more is known about the effects of neck-bands.

Another major point was the importance of having an experienced neck-bander to demonstrate how it should be done. On this trip we have heard a good deal (and seen a bad example) of too tight neck-banding. I suggested a calliper measurement of the neck and graduated marks on the band, numbered with varying diameters within the range of swan collar sizes. Bill said it had never been tried but thought it was quite a good idea. When one remembers how the oesophagus becomes distended with grass or grain one can't help wondering whether a neck-band doesn't inevitably limit the intake when food is plentiful.

TUESDAY 26 FEBRUARY

A miserable start to my day having to say 'Goodbye' to Phil. She and Dafila went off on a bird-watching excursion to the place we had been to when last in Tokyo. The bus sat waiting for ages outside the hotel, and I went into it for a second 'Goodbye', then went upstairs to the room she will stay in for one more night. It makes me *very* unhappy to be separated from her for 10 days. I felt empty – and still do as I write in the 707 on the way to Beijing.

THE FAR EAST SHUTTLE

Sun 24 Feb.'80
Odaito, Hokkaido

Cygnus cygnus

showing supraorbital
glands enlarged
when living
in salt
water

After they'd gone I sat in the hotel room working on the World Conservation Strategy and painting Whooper Swan heads in this book. I wrote Phil a note and left it on the dressing table. At 1300 I took my baggage down, put the room key in my pocket, rigged my suitcase on the trolley and ordered a taxi to take me to the city air terminal. From there I was to take a 'limousine' – actually a perfectly ordinary bus if rather a posh one.

I decided to have lunch at the terminal and caught the bus easily thereafter. It took 70 minutes to get to Narita Airport. There I put my hand in my pocket and found the room key. A kind man at the Information Desk said he would send it back.

Just landed in Peking. A totally new airport building since my last visit in 1979. Outside temperature 2°C. Met by Mrs Ma [EPO interpreter] and Mr Jin Jianming (the quiet authoritative man from the EPO on my last visit). Nancy could be seen among the people waiting at a series of windows. She was in a state when we met as she thought she had left her purse containing 'all our dollars' on the dining room table at the hotel and a call by Mr Jin when they got to the airport had established that there was no trace of it. Naturally she was tremendously concerned and upset – but when we got into the car there was the purse on the back seat! Poor girl, she had clearly suffered considerably in the interim.

So to the Peking Hotel and Room 1218, where we worked on my television speech for next morning which Nancy had drafted for translation, being all that Li Chaobo [then Director of EPO] was not going to say in his.

WEDNESDAY 27 FEBRUARY

Ready by 0800 to go to the Broadcasting Centre. Our hosts were not quite ready for us – could we wait a few minutes in the car, please? Eventually we went round to the back of the rather seedy building to a small room with the ordinary armchair/table set-up and one small camera. Here were assembled most of our Chinese friends – Li Chaobo, Zhang Shuzhong [a Vice-Director of EPO], Wang Menghu (his name means 'dreaming of tiger'), Dr Zhu Jing of the Academy of Sciences (very cordial), and Zhou Xianrong, who went to Manchuria with us last time, and is now promoted a Vice-Director of EPO for Foreign Affairs. Also two new scientists both of whom spoke some English: Dr Wu Zhonglun who is a botanist and high up in the Academia Sinica and Professor Ma Shijun who is an ecologist and studied at Cambridge University; he is high up in the Zoological Institute.

There is no doubt that we have been able to meet most of the influential Chinese scientists, and many of the important administrators in our field of interest. It seems that the Chinese veneration of advanced age has made contact with them – even the younger ones – easier than it might otherwise have been. I am quite encouraged by the impact WWF has made.

THURSDAY 28 FEBRUARY

Flew from Peking to Kwangchow in order to cross the border into Hong Kong by train. I stayed, as twice before, at the Tungfang Hotel.

FRIDAY 29 FEBRUARY

I was called at 0530 to catch the 0815 train to Hong Kong from a station not five minutes from the hotel. There is a new element in the journey since we made it in 1978: the passport, immigration and customs formalities take place in the railway stations at Kwangchow (and Hong Kong) and the train goes straight through. So the time was needed.

The train journey took one and a half hours and was punctuated for me by a minor tummy upset. A television screen showed colour films of people dancing and singing, then a wildlife film of a viverrid which looked like a rufous buff Polecat with a black face. The 'private life' filming was quite good and there was footage on its exploitation for fur and scent gland oil. There was a sequence showing it killing a rattlesnake (*are* there rattlesnakes in Asia?).

I was met at the station and taken by Hilton Mercedes to the Hilton Hotel in Hong Kong, where my room, 1302, was a splendid suite – as last September.

On my way out to lunch I met up with Sylvia Earle [American marine biologist] and later in the evening Sylvia and I went to dinner with Ken Searle who looks after the birds in the Botanical Gardens – as a hobby; he is a doctor. He came to see us at Slimbridge a few years back but has been away from Hong Kong during our two recent visits – last September he was on honeymoon with his journalist wife Sue Earle, who became Sue Searle. Also at the dinner were Chris Huxley and wife Penny, who had bronchitis and was feeling rather ill. Chris Huxley administers Hong Kong's wild-life trade and knows a *lot* about the ivory trade. He could be useful to the SSC. Sue produced a wonderful dinner but it didn't start till 2130 so it was very late by the time Chris Huxley dropped us back at the Hilton. Ken is a very direct person but I get on well with him.

SATURDAY I MARCH

To the Ocean Park – the brain child of Sir Kenneth Ping-Fan Fung. It is in two parts connected by a cable-car service, which we used. In its first 3 years it has had 6 million visitors, and capturing the enthusiasm of youngsters with swings and roundabouts seems to me justified. But it has been criticized for being too much a fun fair and too little educational. There is said to be a basic school education programme but this could be stepped up considerably.

Sylvia and I were first taken by Ted Hammond (who, as a veterinary, runs the animal side of the park) to the laboratories where there were 3 pairs of the local *Tursiops* dolphins. There was also a pretty garden with 2 pairs of Sarus Cranes and a waterfall. In a large cage was a pair of Golden-haired Monkeys – on loan from Peking Zoo – and due to go back in two days. They made a striking exhibit as they are large, unusual and extremely affectionate. There were some mixed white and pink flamingos – though we had too little time to look at them critically.

We took the cable car over to the headland and went to the 'coral atoll' exhibit. It is very good indeed and there was a fine variety of fishes. There were shoals of chaetodons (butterfly fish) including a local one that was new to me: *C. weiberi*. Big Leopard Sharks with Remoras swam round – schools of *Lutjanus* [snappers], *Zanclus* [Moorish Idol], *Heniochus* [coachman], *Siganus* [rabbit fish or spinefeet] and some big *Cheilinus undulatus* [Hump-headed Maori Wrasse]. I thought it all rather well done. We also went behind the scenes where they were breeding lots of *Cromileptes altivelis* [Barramundi], *Chaetodon vagabundus* (maybe locally caught ones) and the Clown Fish, *Amphiprion bicinctus*(?). The 'wave' exhibit had sea lions and penguins and a beach with breaking waves; it is quite excellent and I believe the only one of its kind in the world.

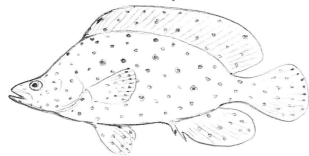

Cromileptes altivelis
Barramundi

Little Grebe
Dalmatian Pelican
Cormorant
Bittern . _Botaurus stellaris_
Chinese Pond Heron
Cattle Egret
Little Egret
Great Egret
Grey Heron
(Purple Heron)
White Ibis
Lesser Spoonbill . _Platalea minor_
European Spoonbill
Common Teal
Garganey
Pintail
Shoveler
Shelduck
Black Kite
Common Buzzard
Imperial Eagle
Steppe Eagle
Marsh Harrier
Osprey
White-breasted Waterhen. _Amaurornis_
phoenicurus
Moorhen
Coot
Little Ringed Plover
Grey Plover
Fantail Snipe . G.gallinago
Eurasian Curlew . _N.arquata_.
Green Sandpiper
Wood Sandpiper
Common Sandpiper
Spotted Redshank
Greenshank
Temminck's Stint
Dunlin
Black-winged Stilt
Herring Gull
Black-headed Gull.
Saunders's Gull . _L. saundersi_.
Spotted Dove. _S. chinensis_
Greater Coucal. _Centropus sinensis_ (heard)
White breasted Kingfisher. _H. smyrnensis_
Common Kingfisher. _Alcedo atthis_

Barn Swallow. Hirundo rustica
Rufous backed Shrike. _L. schach_
also Black Phase.
Chinese Starling. _S. sinensis_
Silky Starling. _S. sericeus_
Grey Starling. _S. cinereus_
Black necked Starling. S. nigricollis
Crested Mynah. _Acridotheres cristatellus_
Magpie. _P pica_
Collared Crow. _Corvus torquatus_
Chinese Bulbul
or Light-vented Bulbul. Pycnonotus sinensis
Black-faced Laughing Thrush _Garrulax_
perspicillatus
Great Reed Warbler. Acrocephalus arundinaceus
Dusky Warbler. _Phylloscopus fuscatus_
Yellow-bellied Wren-Warbler. _Prinia flaviventris_
Fantail Warbler or Zitting Cisticola. _C. juncidis_
Stonechat. _Saxicola torquata_
Dusky Thrush _T. naumanni_
(Grey Thrush T. cardis)
Richards's Pipit. Anthus novaeseelandiae
White Wagtail . _M. alba_
Grey Wagtail _M cinerea_
Yellow Wagtail _M. flava_
Little Bunting. _E pusilla_
Tree Sparrow. _P. montanus_

Introduced now feral:
Rose-ringed Parakeet. _Psittacula krameri_

69 spp seen or heard by me.
+ 2 seen by others in the party.

Common Teal. <u>Anas c. crecca</u> and
Garganey. <u>Anas querquedula</u>.
San Tin. 2.3.80

Peter Scott.

179

Saunders's Gull
Larus saundersi

TUESDAY 4 MARCH

First a World Conservation Strategy press interview and then a television interview in the VIP room at the station. Train to Kwangchow. On the train they showed the Chinese wild Panda film which had been shown some time ago on BBC television. I wrote my speech for the news conference on the World Conservation Strategy.

At Kwangchow we were bused to the airport for the flight to Peking, which ended at the new terminal building, and a ride on the very long passenger conveyor belt. Then to the Peking Hotel once more.

SPEECH NOTES FOR THE PEKING LAUNCH OF THE WORLD CONSERVATION STRATEGY.

W.C.S. (Start)   ①

The <u>object</u> of DEVELOPMENT is to provide for **social and economic** welfare.

The object of CONSERVATION is to ensure the planets capacity to **sustain** development and to **continue** to support life.

THE W⁄C⁄S⁄ shows, for perhaps the first time, that
CONS. is ~~shown to be~~ an aid to DEVPMt.
and that DEVPmt is ~~shown to be~~ an essential element in CONS.

NEED FOR A CONS. STRATEGY in a GLOBAL <u>WAR ON WASTE</u> and <u>UNNECESSARY DESTRUCTION</u>.

A COMMON STRATEGY involving COOPERATION between CONSERVATIONISTS and DEVELOPERS

Despite the efforts of conservationists over the last thirty years, the destruction for short term gain goes on virtually unchecked..... (examples opposite)

← We should establish <u>three essential criteria</u>:
1. The EXTENT of the LOSS that is occurring or is about to occur.
2. The IMMINENCE of the loss or damage.
3. The CHANCES of preventing the loss for a significant time.

<u>PRIORITIES</u>   (over)

* <u>TRF</u> : 30 hectares per min (= 75 acres)
  Lowland rainforests going even faster.
  Lowland forests of Malaysia Indonesia & the
  Philippines gone by 2,000 — A loss without precedent
  in recorded history.

* <u>Desertification</u>: More than $\frac{1}{3}$ of land surface is already
  desert or semi-desert. 19% more about to go.

* <u>Wetlands</u>, <u>Estuaries</u> & <u>Shallow Seas</u>: drainage,
  dredging, dumping, pollution, & 'shore improvement'?

* <u>Erosion & Loss of fertile land</u>

* <u>XTN of SPP</u>   1000 Vertebrates
                     Unknown number of invertebrates
                     25,000 spp of Plants.

* <u>Genetic Diversity</u> of domestic animals &
                        crop plants.

* <u>Depleted Fisheries</u>   25 of worlds major fisheries
                           are seriously depleted

This list of waste & destruction is only part of
a much larger problem. We don't seem yet to
have learnt HOW to conserve — or if we have,
we haven't passed our lessons on to others.

We must adopt a strategy — <u>a World</u>
<u>Conservation Strategy</u> to win the war
<u>against thoughtless</u> destruction & waste

PRIORITIES

The longer we leave it, the more costly to repair damage.

☐ Man's dependence on habitat or species.

☐ Give priority to spp with low reproductive potential.

☐ Tackle the problem before the 'point of no return' is reached.

☐ Deal with causes not symptoms

Four basic human problems :
① There is a lack of **facts**. (Gaps in our knowledge)
② There is a lack of **understanding** even when the facts are known.
③ There is a lack of **will**.
④ In most developing countries there is a lack of **money**.

The **money** must be provided
The **will** to conserve will emerge with greater **knowledge and understanding**.
The DECISION MAKERS, & those who advise them, must develop the **will** and the **vision** to act.
The WCS' has indicated guide lines, but a new generation comes along every 25 years — so the need to communicate is unending, The effectiveness of law and policy must be continuously reassessed.
The Strategy will need continuous UPDATING

CONS is most urgently needed where UNDERDEVELOPMENT prevents any real understanding of the need.

So DEVELOPMENT is the dominating prerequisite ~~for~~ GLOBAL CONSERVAT^N.

CHINA:
- March to be Month of CONS. EDUCAT^N.
- China's CONTRIBUT^N to WORLD CONS.
- China's TREE PLANTING.

- Whales & Whaling. IWC Membership.

ECO-DEVELOPMENT provides mans basic needs & satisfies his cultural aspirations, without depleting resources or destroying the systems that support life.

ECO-D⁻ conserves rather than depletes
maintains rather than degrades
the quality of air, soil & water.
exploits indigenous materials & skills.
evolves with the help of the people
aims to meet their needs rather than generate profits ~~for~~ others. (involved)

ECO-D needs a new kind of aid & a world order that respects the economic independence of communities as well as their rights to political self-determination.

WEDNESDAY 5 MARCH

Quiet morning devoted to the translation of my speech at the news conference, and writing up. Lars and Cary Lindblad came to my room and later we went for lunch together – of which he became host. They are negotiating for other travel agencies who, they complain, are so brash and have no idea about common courtesies with the Chinese. They spend their time smoothing out umbrage. They are staying at the Government Guest House, which they say is *very quiet*.

In the afternoon Mr Qin came to say Vice-Premier Gu Mu would receive us on Friday.

THURSDAY 6 MARCH

Lunch in the old building of the hotel – Sichuan/Hunan food – with T. C. Wu, the influential Hong Kong journalist, who is wonderfully good company. Also at lunch was Martine Cartier-Bresson, young wife of the famous photographer and daughter of Louis Franck (WWF Treasurer), and Nancy Nash. The afternoon was spent getting speeches ready for the WCS news conference and the subsequent banquet. Translations with Xiao Ma (the first word pronounced shau – literally 'little Ma') who is marvellous, and Mr Ge who is rather trying. At 1800 Room 5 off the bar was packed with people. All the EPO people, a large number of journalists and a strong contingent from UNESCO.

FRIDAY 7 MARCH

Caroline Blunden – twin sister of Jane B – came to see me in my room at 0900. She is studying at the Central Academy of Fine Art. I showed her the Huang Zhou book which she flicked through. She had never heard of him or of Xu (pronounced shu) Linlu, the famous painter of shrimps, but she said 'they all draw so well'. She has been here on her own for eight months. Like her sister she's rather impressive in terms of *doing* things. I liked her. She wanted to know whether a search of remnant populations of Przewalski's Horse in China could be initiated. It is something that might be considered later, but this is not the moment for new ideas in our relationship with our Chinese colleagues.

Went to see Vice-Premier Gu Mu (pronounced Gu Moo) in the Great Hall of the People. We were a little late and we were rushed in to find them all standing just inside the door, ready to take the group photograph.

I congratulated the Vice-Premier on his recent election to the secretariat of the Central Committee of the Party. This makes him one of the Top Ten. He was a quiet, gentle little man. I told him all about the WCS and its simultaneous launch all over the world. He finally asked, 'Is there anything you want which I could help you to achieve?'. I said that it was all going forward very smoothly thanks to the cordial relations, but of course if he could put in a good word for wildlife conservation in general and pandas in particular that would be very good.

My last point was to reiterate the splendid cooperation of the EPO and we took our leave. We had had more than 50 minutes.

I hope I have managed to conceal my personal reservations about the WCS document. To my way of thinking its materialistic message (conservation is for financial self-interest) should have been balanced by a strong ethical and aesthetic pitch which could have put it onto a much higher philosophical plane – and therefore made it a much more lastingly influential document. I went on about this a good deal at the drafting stage. Instead it seems that the editorial committee was afraid of putting off the Third World pragmatists with airy-fairy conservation ethics. To me the final document seems to lack a soul. We are told it will be periodically up-dated. A soul needs to be breathed into it, and this could still be done, if they really mean to keep it up to the minute. I wonder if they will.

SATURDAY 8 MARCH

At 1130 I went to the home of the painter Huang Zhou – one of China's most famous living painters. (His name is pronounced Wang Jo.) His flat – very small – is in a large seedy tenement block not too far from the centre of the city. The 'studio' is a tiny room, with the walls covered with his prints, and a large glass case full of small sculpture and pottery – all in perfect taste. At the window end was a small extension to another window making a kind of conservatory with some potted trees. There were hanging bird cages, but the two pairs of birds – Peking Robins and White Canaries (known as White Jade Birds) – were not in them. They were hopping in the bushes and free to come into the main part of the room. Mrs Huang was on crutches, having an ankle in plaster after a bicycle accident.

I gave him two small originals – one of Pintails with reeds (which Huang said was a nice composition, 'rather like a Chinese painting') and the other of a family of three Bewick's Swans. Huang got down some donkey prints and a book of his animal drawings, on both of which he wrote.

By any standards Huang Zhou is a great draughtsman. He is famous for drawing donkeys. During the Cultural Revolution, under the Gang of Four, he was told, 'You draw donkeys – you can work like a donkey,' so he was made to pull a cart. He had to wear a wooden board declaring he was a useless artist. For ten years he was not allowed to paint. Many of his paintings are 'party political' with lots of smiling faces. He likes to draw women, and some of his faces are hauntingly beautiful. His bird drawings are full of movement. Oh yes, he can draw.

He is crippled with rheumatoid arthritis brought on by the rigours of his donkey days when he worked in water and was required to walk up to 35 kilometres per day. His treatment is said to have included 'torture'. He walks with a stick and requires an arm to lean on, but he is an ebullient character with a forceful manner of speech, and is evidently hugely respected.

Later we went down to the waiting taxi and went to lunch. Nancy had invited Martine Cartier-Bresson and we were joined by the artist Xu Linlu and Yang Diyang (the German-speaking Chinese journalist). Huang was greeted by the Peking Hotel manager who insisted that we should have a private dining room.

Huang had a special relationship with all the waiters, and later came a middle-aged waitress (or maybe a cook) who had befriended him in his exile; he talked a lot to her with many jokes. There was a fairly continuous stream of people coming in to talk to him. The gentle Xu Linlu was evidently much less famous although he was a student of Qi Baishi – the best known Chinese painter of the previous generation. Both Xu and Huang were friends of Vice-Premier Gu Mu so I added a PS to the letter of thanks to him telling him about the lunch, and how we had toasted him.

After a good many *mao tai ganbeis* (Chinese for 'bottoms up'), I had to explain that I had work still to do in the afternoon. 'That's alright,' said Huang Zhou, 'we must always help our friends,' and promptly sank my *mao tai* as well as his own.

I presented a little drawing of a Tree Sparrow to Xu Linlu and while I was writing on it for him, an argument developed over who should pay for the lunch. I had earlier established that we were to be the hosts, but now the decision was reversed and there was nothing we could do about it. 'We may be poor,' said Huang Zhou 'but not so poor that we can't entertain our honoured guests at lunch.' Soon after he left. My lasting impression of Huang Zhou is that he is a great man.

Then up to Room 1211 to have our final meeting with the EPO before the long journey home – 26 hours if all goes well.

On the way back I bought a small carpet in Karachi airport for Phil for US$180. It is *quite* nice. I *hope* she'll like it.

CHAPTER 7

Panda Country

DIARY 39 1980

Oriental Cuckoo
Cuculus saturatus

The objects of my sixth visit to China were once more World Wildlife Fund business and to establish George Schaller, from the New York Zoological Society, in his long-term study of the Giant Panda. Secondly, we wanted to see panda country and if we were very lucky, a wild Giant Panda. The third object was to persuade the People's Republic of China to join the International Whaling Commission, hopefully before the July meetings in England. Further objectives were to encourage the PRC to ratify CITES and to get them to join IUCN and IWRB. We also hoped to get agreement on additional conservation projects in China in due course. We had a list of the endangered Chinese species with us.*

Towards all these things I was eager to meet the new Prime Minister, Zhao Ziyang, and maybe also the Deputy Prime Minister, Gu Mu, once more.

SATURDAY 10 MAY 1980
Left Slimbridge at 1400. Rather less unfinished business than usual although I have only been home for a week since our three-part trip to 'save the whales' by chairing the 16-nation Indian Ocean Alliance meeting in the Seychelles, to have a holiday swimming and diving on the coral reefs of D'Arros in the Amirante Islands and to chair the SSC meeting at Kilaguni Lodge in Kenya. Phil went home after the first two.

MONDAY 12 MAY
Arrived in Beijing. There had been some confusion about when we were due to arrive and we found that Nancy [Nash] and George [Schaller] had gone off to Chengdu in Sichuan province and would await our arrival on the next day.

---

* Endangered Chinese species: White Crested Ibis, Red-Crowned Crane, Black-necked Crane, Chinese Merganser, Mandarin Duck, Lesser White-fronted Goose, *Crossoptilon manchuricum* and other Pheasants, *Ciconia boyciana*, Tiger, Giant and Lesser Panda, Golden-backed Monkey and other primates, Yangtse River Dolphin (*Lipotes*), Père David's Deer, Asian Elephant, Snow Leopard, Yangtse Crocodile and Alligator. Endangered Plants.

In the afternoon Phil and I decided to go once more to the beautiful Forbidden City, particularly for her to get pictures of the Wall of Nine Dragons, which has been a favourite of ours since we first saw it in 1978.

TUESDAY 13 MAY

There to meet us at the airport in Chengdu were George, Nancy, Mrs Ma [EPO interpreter] and Yang Rudai, Deputy Governor of Sichuan, and Cheng Hua, the EPO Director for Sichuan. Whilst still at the airport Nancy met some friends who were a delegation from the Dalai Lama on the way to Lhasa. She went off to talk to them, which drew black looks from those greeting us. The car which took

The Wall of Nine Dragons at the Forbidden City

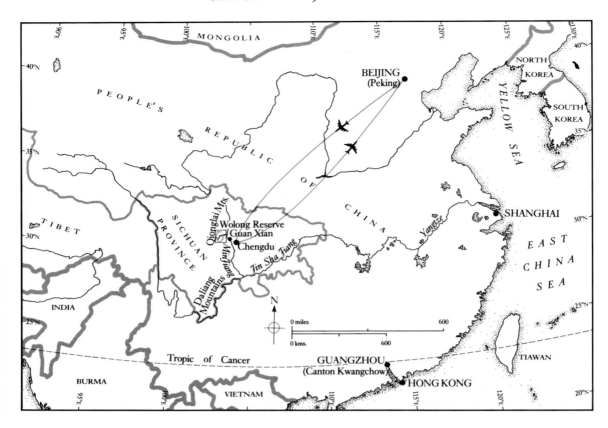

us to the Jin Jiang Hotel with the Deputy Governor had black net curtains.

In the afternoon we were taken to see the nine pandas in the Chengdu Zoo. Four of the pandas were in two very small cages with bars on all four sides. The door between the two was open. One – said to be female – was pacing up and down like a caged tiger. The other three were being fed in the second cage. The three together seemed to have a peck order but there were occasional noisy warnings. Food was bamboo, apples and, we were told, sugar.

The other adult was not in evidence. One of the young was persuaded to come out into an outdoor enclosure (very reluctantly) by a lady who tapped it on the head, whereupon it turned a somersault. It was completely conditioned to this, and progressed with the motion of a hoop. This was amusing to the Chinese people watching but sad to us.

That evening the Deputy Governor held a dinner in a big room on the top floor of our hotel. In the middle of the evening a party broke up from some tables behind screens in one corner of the room to disclose among the guests our old friend Lars Eric Lindblad

Wolong

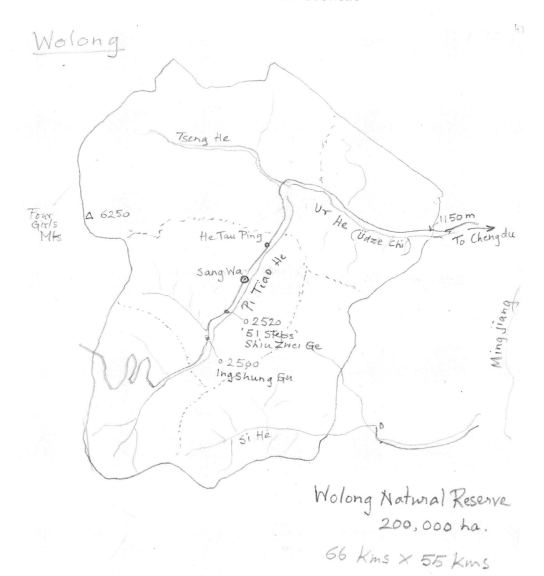

Tseng He

Four Girls Mts

△ 6250

He Tau Ping

Sang Wa

Pi Tiao He

Ur He (Üdze Chi)

1150 m

To Chengdu

Ming Jiang

o 2520
'51 Steps'
Shiu Zhei Ge

o 2560
Ing Shung Gu

Si He

Wolong Natural Reserve
200,000 ha.

66 Kms × 55 Kms

Pi Tiao He 61 km long.
Rainy season: July – Sept. Dec – Mar. dry season
Temp. Av. 7.8 C Highest 26° Lowest −11.5°
Annual Rain 1060 mm. Humidity. Av. 80%
No frost 180 days.

Thamnolaea leucocephala
The River Chat.
× ⅔

and his wife Cary – to the mutual amazement of us all! They were leading a tour to Lhasa. The dinner did not last too long, in spite of much *mao tai* and many speeches.

WEDNESDAY 14 MAY
We set off in a minibus from Chengdu (pronounced Chungdu) stopping at Guan Xian for lunch. Just north of the city we stopped at the 'Tu Kin' temple* which stands on the eastern bank of the Min Jiang by a most impressive bridge. Both date from AD 497. Here too one can see an irrigation scheme that is 2,200 years old. It watered 570,000 hectares and was begun in the Qin Dynasty around 200 BC.

Then on to Wolong (pronounced Wulong or Wulung). It is one of China's 45 Natural Reserves and covers 200,000 hectares of steep valleys at the eastern foot of the Qionglai Mountains which lie to the west of the upper reaches of the Min Jiang. Wolong is in the south-west part of Wenchuan County, in Sichuan Province. Within the Reserve the Four Girls Mountain rises to 6,250 metres, and Mount Balang, 5,000 metres high, is in the western part of it. Both are snow-covered all the year round. They told us that the

* We learned long afterwards that what we took to be a Chinese name 'Tu Kin' was in fact a translation for us into English. 'Er Wang Miao' means the Temple of the Two Kings.

<u>Wed 14</u>. Chengtu (pronounced Chungdu) 500 m. a.s.l.
with minibus through Kwang Tsien ^{Guan Xian} ~~$~~ for
lunch. Tu Kin temple by bridge ~~Sung Dynasty~~ 497 AD.
    Divided river : Min Chiang feeding Yangtse.
    Irrigation scheme 2,200 years old. Ching Dynasty 250 BC.
        570,000 ha. irrigated.
Then on to Wolong (Wulong, Wulung)
    Large & comfortable guest house at Sang Wa
Banquet. Too much food. Many speeches.
                        Pleasant welcome.
                            Birds on the way.
                            White breasted
                                    Kingfisher
                            Shrike
                            Swallow.

Da Shong Mau
Giant Panda.

Seen on the way up the Ming jiang :

Plumbeous Redstart.
River Chat.
Large billed Crow.
Pied Wagtail

'The Fifty-One Steps' Day: on the way up

mammals in the Reserve include Giant Panda, Golden-haired Monkey, Takin, White-lipped Deer, Musk Deer and Tufted Deer.

It was dusk when we arrived at Sang Wa – originally a timber extraction factory – and were driven to a large and comfortable guest house. Our rooms at Sang Wa were quite comfortable but they had prepared for our coming at fairly short notice and the bathrooms – a row of them – had only just been completed. It was a chilly evening and we all decided to have nice hot baths before dinner. What we did not discover until we pulled out the plug was that the plug hole had not been connected to the drain, so the whole bath ran out on to the floor. Unfortunately all the other bathrooms were in the same state and each one of the party learned the problem the hard way. The bathroom wing became totally flooded – and remained so more or less throughout our stay, so that when we used it we had to put on rubber boots. At 5,000 feet the climate was pretty cool and very damp.

Tired and travel-stained as we were, there was no way in which we could avoid a banquet with, as usual, too much food, and many speeches. But their welcome was pleasant and heart-warming. Birds seen on the way up included White-breasted Kingfisher and Shrike Swallow.

Saturnid Moth
× ½

THURSDAY 15 MAY

The 'Fifty-One Steps' Day. We all went by minibus 5 kilometres up the Pi Tiao He (the last word is pronounced as a short 'her' and means 'river'). Then a long climb of 500 metres which took us 2 hours and 40 minutes to 'May 1 Observing Spot'. Signs of Giant Pandas to look out for: old droppings, fresh droppings,* chewed bamboo shoots, paths through bush. (All of them had been seen by the end of the day – except the creatures themselves.)

Few birds were seen, but flycatchers were heard most, warblers seen briefly, and an Oriental Cuckoo (*Cuculus saturatus*) was heard.

Discussion before lunch: *George Schaller*: Must learn something about pandas *before* trying radio tracking. *Wang Menghu*: We know all that can be learnt without radio tracking. Would like to use radio tracking soonest. 5 people have observed pandas for $2\frac{1}{2}$ years. *George Schaller*: Radio equipment must be designed; we must consider Action Plan. Some discussion of tranquillization techniques. Radio duration 6–12 months. Results not so good in forest.

After lunch of buns and hard-boiled eggs we walked further along a path into panda habitat – 3 species of lichens, *Berberis* etc. The descent took about an hour.

---

* Before setting out from Beijing the Chinese had told us they could not guarantee to show us wild pandas but they could absolutely guarantee to show us fresh droppings.

Overleaf: Looking down on the valley in which runs the Pi Tiao He

River Chat *Thamnolaea leucocephala*
     (Chaimorrornis)

Plumbeous Redstart *Rhyacornis fuliginosus.*

Cuculus.
sparverioides
Large Hawk Cuckoo.
Drawn later

FRIDAY 16 MAY

Rain early. The bird call we have been unable to identify – bird not seen – is the Large Hawk-Cuckoo (*Cuculus sparverioides*).

We spent the morning indoors with a conference and briefing.

In the afternoon we drove down the valley in the rain to look at the site for the new Research Centre. The place is called Hetao Ping, which means Walnut Terrace. The main laboratories (800 square metres) will be on the Terrace. The other 1,800 square metres of the development – living accommodation for the scientists – will be below the road beside the river – the Pi Tiao He.

There was a small nursery for trees. In it was *Chimonobambusa szechuanensis*; this is a bamboo grown from seed brought from the

4

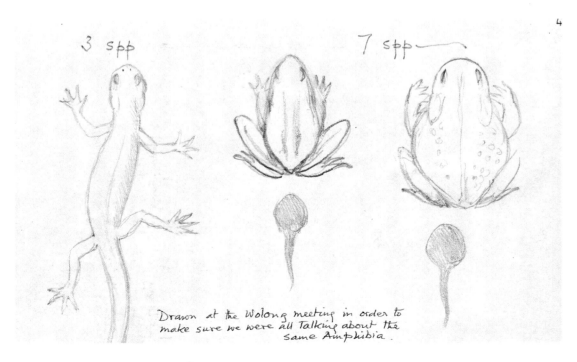

3 spp   7 spp

Drawn at the Wolong meeting in order to make sure we were all Talking about the same Amphibia.

Some moths which came to the
lights at Sang Wa. 1900 m.
in May 1980

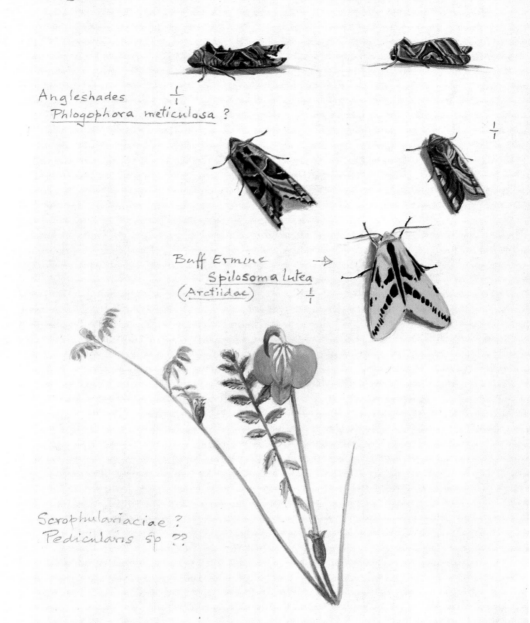

Angleshades $\frac{1}{1}$
  Phlogophora meticulosa ?

$\frac{1}{1}$

Buff Ermine →
  Spilosoma lutea
(Arctiidae) $\times \frac{1}{1}$

Scrophulariaciae ?
  Pedicularis sp ??

Senior
Vice Dir.

NOTES ON MEETING a.m. 16th May 1980.
at Sang Wa

Tsao Tsang Gwei
Chief Warden of Wolong

200,000 ha.

Main Tasks:
1. Implement new Env. Protection Law + new Forestry Law.
   Education. Prevent fire
               Pest control.
               Prevent erosion.
2. Biological Studies of rare spp. especially Giant Panda
   'Rationally make use of all natural resources'
3. Captive Pandas. Like domestic animals.
       Domesticate.
   Study breeding in wild + captivity.
4. Scientific Surveys. Scientists and their students.
   Exchange info.
   Invite foreign experts for exchange of info.
   Educational programs — Universities. Institutes of
                                        Zoo. Botany etc.

Wolong Reserve
(Wulung) lies at eastern end of Qionglai Mts.
         upper reaches Mingjiang River in the
         SE part of Wung Chow County.
   E−W 54 kilometers. N−S 66 kms.

Av. Temp. 7.8°C Highest 26°C. Lowest −11.5°C
Annual Rain 1060 ·   180

Mammals c.100 spp
Birds c.200 spp. (Some migratory)

10 spp of Pheasants. Lophophorus sclateri
Tragopan Temminckii
Crossoptilon
4-5 spp fishes in river. Tetraogallus
10 spp Amphibia   7 frogs 3 Salamanders .
29 spp protected living in reserve .

1st Category 4 ⎤   ⎧ 1st No hunting
2nd   "   7 ⎬ Rare spp ⎨ 2nd Central Govt
3rd   "   18 ⎦   ⎨   Control of
                                ⎨   Provincial Govt.
                                ⎨ 3rd   "   "   "
                                ⎩   Planned "harvesting"

1st Giant Panda .
     Golden Haired Monkey   In Wolong — all
     White-Lipped Deer C. albirostris   animals protected —
     Takin   even those in no category.
2nd Lesser Panda
     Snow Leopard .

4,000 spp of plants.
   Red Cedar — Unique to Sichuan . Tsuga dumosa
   Cloud Cedar   Taxus chinensis
   'Red bean' Cedar. Larix mastersiana .

               Cercidiphyllum japonicum var. sinense
               Tetracentron sinense
               Dipteronia sinensis.

Daliang Mountains (which lie on the north side of the Jin Sha River) – a Panda Reserve. It is an autumn food for pandas, but does not at present grow in Wolong Reserve. The experimental plot has been set up to discover how long this bamboo takes to grow in the Pi Tiao He valley.

In a thick scrub was a very loud and beautiful bird call – very close but the bird was totally invisible. According to Professor Hu Jinchu, who is an excellent field naturalist, it was *Cettia fortipes* (*montanus*) the Brownish-flanked Bush-Warbler.

SATURDAY 17 MAY

A steepish climb from the road to Yingxiong Gu – which is pronounced Ing Shung Gu and means Hero's Valley – up a path that had been used for timber extraction. I climbed 500 metres in 1 hour and 10 minutes, passing through 4 tunnels. On arrival my pulse rate was taken (160) by our peripatetic lady physician – who has an air cushion full of oxygen. Later she took my blood pressure and it had gone down to 130/80.

Further climb to the panda enclosure. ('Only a few steps' but it was at least another $\frac{1}{2}$ kilometre.) The building contained barred cages of small size with 5 adult pandas in them. We went out into the $1\frac{1}{2}$-hectare enclosure with 2 baby pandas who were scared stiff,

Dr George Schaller with a young Giant Panda, Wolong Reserve

Da Shong Mau
at Inchong Gu.
17. 5. 80

and at once ran into the bushes. They were caught and carried back, were perched on a log and remained there only very briefly. Some pictures were taken with me and George Schaller close to one of them, but none without people. As the last one went off through the scrub, a few fleeting glimpses were possible, and Phil and I clicked our cameras, but it was an unhappy business for the panda cubs. Eventually one of them, terrified, found a hole and went into it – with up to a dozen people all round it. By this time it was covered with black earth and so frightened that we persuaded everyone to come away and stop pestering it. Throughout the whole incident there was evidence of fairly rough handling and very low standards of sensitivity towards the feelings of the animals. The two baby pandas were only caught 10 days ago.

SUNDAY 18 MAY

A long bus ride up the valley to the high mountains which were draped with cloud. As we followed the course of the Pi Tiao the vegetation changed and new rhododendrons in flower began to

3 Lammergeiers
Gypaetus
barbatus

Long legged Buzzard
Buteo rufinus

Griffon Vulture
Gyps fulvus ?

Ashy-throated Warbler ?
Phylloscopus maculipennis
At 9,000 ft in Wolong
Reserve
Sichuan.
18.5.80

Citrine Wagtail
  Motacilla citreola

18.5.80. Pi Tiao He Valley.
Flock of 30-40

appear. Then the road began to double back on itself and zigzag up the steep mountainside. This was above the bamboo scrub and therefore above the panda line.

There were fine old conifers of at least 3 species – enormous old trees in scattered groups. At this stage it looked as though the cloud would clear and we might get up to the pass, but finally at a little over 10,000 feet our minibus had trouble getting us up the hill. We walked up to the next corner which was a good look-out.

Below us wisps of cloud were forming and rising in quite strong thermals. In one of these a large bird of prey was circling. It was pale with a wedge-shaped tail – a Lammergeier. Presently it was joined by two more – one equally pale, the third darker, perhaps immature. We watched them circling far below us, in and out of the wisps of cloud, showing pale against the dark forest of pines and evergreen oak. At a later stage we saw two buzzards (probably *Buteo rufinus*) the Long-legged Buzzard, as they were quite russet in colour, and two Griffon Vultures – one below us with pale grey back and wings showing well, and black primaries and secondaries.

I had a good view of an Ashy-throated Warbler, *Phylloscopus maculipennis*, with yellow rump and two wing bars (whitish) and we

Unidentified
Eagle circling

heard a Large-billed Crow, but on the whole there were disappointingly few birds. It was decided to abandon the climb in the minibus because of the low cloud and the frozen snow on the road. We turned back and stopped at a guard post where we met a painter who showed us his sketch book. His name was Sang Daguo and he painted the oil paintings on the walls of the house we are staying in.

It was after lunch that I climbed up through the scrub to photograph some of the rhododendrons. This no doubt was when my leech attached itself and sucked my blood undisturbed during the bus ride home. We came upon a flock of Citrine Wagtails not far from Sang Wa. When I got out of the minibus the fully fed leech must have fallen on the floor, where, without knowing it, I trod on it. After walking 50 yards back down the road to see the Citrine Wagtails, I returned to the bus to find some pandemonium about the pool of blood on the bus floor beneath the seat I had been sitting in. I was still quite unaware that it was my blood. When I pulled up my trouser leg there was a trickle of blood from just below the knee, which took some hours to dry up.

In the evening Zhou Xiaozhou painted pandas for us, and we had a banquet at which we were hosts.

MONDAY 19 MAY

Phil and I travelled from Sang Wa to Chengdu with Cheng Hua and Xiao Ma in the EPO Director's car (with curtained windows!). It was a bright sunny day, and a tragedy to be unable to use it to see the high mountains which had been in the clouds yesterday.

A bird with a windswept crest – brown with a whitish breast and belly – sat on a telephone wire. Was it a Puff-throated Bulbul, a Mountain Bulbul, a Brown Shrike, a Collared Finchbill, or a female Greater Racket-tailed Drongo? I am fairly sure it was a bulbul.

Bulbul-size

TUESDAY 20 MAY

Awoke after good night's rest in Jin Jiang Hotel, Chengdu. Dry and warm! In the garden by the pond: Great Reed Warbler, Brown Shrike, Tree Sparrow.

First to the bank to cash £80 and US$60 of Phil's to bail us all out. Then a short walk in the garden of the hotel, where Small Whites were feeding from flowers of Comfrey, and Great Reed Warblers were singing.

Then to an interminable meeting in our hotel room at which Wang Menghu held forth on how he needed 2.81 million Yuan to build his Research Station in Wolong. It was clearly an exercise in 'Empire Building', but it emerged that the Chinese system demanded something of this kind as a launching pad for the panda project.

In vain did George and I say that the initial field research could be quite cheap, that observing and understanding in the field led most quickly to scientific discovery, and this process was achieved by people, not by buildings.

WEDNESDAY 21 MAY
Flew back to Peking, and established ourselves again in the Peking Hotel.

Peter Scott, Sang Daguo, Shau Ma and the sketch book

THURSDAY 22 MAY
We began the interminable meetings with the EPO people again at about 0915. After 'Did-you-sleep-wells' Wang Menghu said he would like to continue with details of the equipment needed for the laboratories etc for the proposed research centre.

I said, 'Would you like to hear the results of the telephone call we have had with our HQ in Switzerland?' He said 'yes' and I made a statement:

'The developments in Wolong consist of seven items. First there are the three separate proposals for captive breeding of pandas.
1. The main breeding "farm" at Hetao Ping (Walnut Terrace) where control of up to 10 individual pandas will be complete, but where the animals will have larger dens, with out-door enclosures, than at Yingxiong Gu (Hero's Valley).
2. The semi-natural enclosure round the spring of up to three hectares which could hold up to three pandas with part of the spring able to be visited by wild pandas – possibly including swing door to admit wild males for mating with captive females.
3. Improvement (without enlargement) of the existing breeding accommodation and enclosure at Yingxiong Gu.

193

The covered way at Beihai Park

Then there is:

4. Building of laboratories.

5. Building of accommodation for research workers and infra-structure.

6. Increased electrical supply for Research Centre.

7. Vehicle bridge across Pi Tiao He (if necessary).

For all of these things, I understand the World Wildlife Fund is prepared to offer a sum of US$1 million to the PRC. The timing will be:

194

Before the end of September 1980 US$400,000
Before the end of September 1981 US$400,000
Before the end of September 1982 US$200,000
_____

US$1,000,000

The above sum is separate from expenses under existing agreements for "field research" vehicles, travel to and from China by Chinese and foreign research workers.

Conditions for this offer are:

1. Close consultation on design of breeding enclosures, with foreign experts.

2. Admission to Wolong of a limited number of carefully selected donors of large sums of money to the project. This *need* not be before 1982.'

There was surprisingly little reaction to the offer of a $1 million donation. The faces seemed as long as ever!

We proceeded to discuss equipment which was listed by our ornithologist friend, Professor Hu Jinchu. The list was so long and expensive that at one stage George Schaller asked if we were going to set up a *University* in Wolong.

We finally broke for lunch. George joined Phil and me and we went to the Sichuan Restaurant in the old hotel. Phil had spent a photographic morning at Beihai Park.

During the lunch break Nancy told Xiao Ma that we had been rather surprised at the lack of reaction to our offer of $1 million.

When the meeting began again Zhang Shuzhong (a Vice-Director of the EPO) became the spokesman. After explaining that he had been away he said he had heard that there had been hard bargaining and there had been a very successful outcome to the negotiations. Everyone on the Chinese side was very pleased with the results and very grateful to the World Wildlife Fund. This was then repeated in speeches by Wang Menghu and Zhou Xianrong (foreign affairs division of EPO).

Then a new problem arose. If the building was to start at the beginning of 1981 then the designs for the breeding station would have to be made by the civil engineer at once. There would be no time to consult experts or even to discuss the installations with Zhao Shicheng (from the Chengdu Zoo), who had been with us, and who spoke quite good English. Considering how *terrible* the barred cages at Yingxiong Gu were we felt it was absolutely essential to get expert advice and try to get someone to come out and go to Wolong very soon.

George said that he would telephone Bill Conway (his boss at the New York Zoological Society) this evening. (He got through later and Bill agreed to come for a week. This is marvellous news.) The meeting ended quite early on a very positive note.

On the whole there seems to be general approval of our decision to give the Chinese a million dollars in order to get the panda project rolling. It has been a fairly heavy responsibility!

FRIDAY 23 MAY

George and I worked on possible plans for the Hetao Ping installations. We are to send observation hide designs for use in watching pandas – in captivity and also in the wild if suitable attractants – 'baiting for pandas' – can be found.

Soon after the first sketch was drawn it was time for us to go down to our room on the 11th floor, pick up our bags and go off in two cars to the airport.

At the airport moderate chaos reigned, but eventually we were checked in and went up for a light lunch in the restaurant.

And so off to our plane – a DC10 – with much waving. The flight was circuitous so as not to fly over South Korea, and we landed first at Osaka.

At Tokyo we were held up by a security search after *dis*embarking. An Italian group travelling first class 'cut up rough' about the thoroughness of the search, which only made it more thorough and slowed down the whole process. One particular Italian became furious and sarcastic – even quite funny – but it doesn't pay.

After some gin and tonic we felt rather better and finally boarded our 747 for London via Anchorage.

CONCLUSIONS ABOUT MY SIXTH AND PHIL'S THIRD VISIT TO CHINA

1. We have successfully launched George Schaller in his project which holds the best chance of any to learn what long-term steps have to be taken to prevent the extinction of the Giant Panda in its wild habitat, and to breed it more successfully in captivity.

2. We have helped to enable the EPO and the Forestry Ministry to establish the Research Station in Wolong which, given the system of government in China, is an essential prerequisite to all scientific work by foreign scientists in the PRC.

3. We have assured a reasonable and practical design for the captive-breeding facilities in Wolong.

4. We have cemented the friendships we have cultivated during our previous visits.

5. We have achieved agreement on all major issues involved in the protocols and action plan for the Panda Studies in Sichuan.

6. We have progressed the plans for close contact between Chinese scientists and administrators and the international conservation community.

7. On a number of occasions deadlock seemed imminent. The diplomacy of Nancy and Phil was of utmost importance in several critical situations.

8. George Schaller's determination to work closely with Chinese scientists, and his frequent references to this essential element in the planning, was an important factor in reaching agreement.

9. Nancy's amazing energy and stamina was another major factor.

10. The follow-up by the World Wildlife Fund and IUCN will have to be meticulously and energetically pursued if the momentum is to be maintained.

11. There were a number of objectives which were not achieved and will require further effort on our part. We are not yet certain whether the PRC will join the International Whaling Commission in time for this year's meeting.

They have not yet undertaken to join CITES, IUCN or IWRB, nor have they yet agreed to discuss with us what help we could give them in order to conserve their other endangered species.

12. Finally I did not get to see the Prime Minister, Zhao Ziyang.

SATURDAY 24 MAY

After an hour at Anchorage and another 45 minutes for 'repairing navigational equipment', we took off on the $8\frac{1}{2}$-hour flight to London.

Postscript 1986. At subsequent meetings of WWF in Switzerland, during the months which followed our visit, our agreement came in for a good deal of criticism, but with hindsight and in spite of the large sum of money involved, I believe it was a worthwhile initiative, and brought a new attitude to conservation in China.

They joined the International Whaling Commission the year after our last visit and played a very significant part in whale conservation. Later they joined both IUCN and CITES but have not yet joined IWRB.

They have made plans for the conservation of their other endangered species; and, of course, they have adopted the World Conservation Strategy.

CHAPTER 8

Coral Fish and Butterflies

DIARY 45   1981

In 1981 the International Union for Conservation of Nature and Natural Resources decided to award me their prestigious John Phillips Medal and Phil and I planned to go to their General Assembly in New Zealand. We thought it would be a good opportunity to visit a number of friends in far-away places on the way there and back. Thus our travels took us to Hong Kong, to Heron Island on the Great Barrier Reef for a week with our friends Ron and Valerie Taylor, and to Christchurch to receive the medal. On the way back Ron and Val took us out from Sydney to a beautiful farm in the 'outback' belonging to Val's brother. After a few days in Australia we went again to Hong Kong to see the wonderful Mai Po Marshes which we had briefly visited by helicopter in 1964 and where I had spent another day bird watching in 1980 (see pages 164–165). On this, our third visit, it seemed we might be able to progress the plans we had proposed on our first visit for some sort of Wildfowl Reserve with conservation and education objectives. My second visit, on which I listed 69 species of birds, had persuaded me that this was a bird habitat of world importance. Departure on such a journey not unnaturally leads to a pious effort to bring a host of half-finished projects to completion before leaving.

WEDNESDAY 7 OCTOBER 1981
The last few days have been fantastically rushed. Pictures and drawings to finish before departure, a foreword outline to be pre-prepared for the Wildfowl Trust President. A quantity of WWF issues to be resolved. Plans for the creation of a Peace Park in the Sinai Peninsula with a letter from Prince Philip to President Sadat. Cassandra Phillips, my new Wildlife Personal Assistant (wife of Adrian P. – formerly IUCN second-in-command), has been preparing the details.

I went to London yesterday for the annual meeting of the Conder Trust. (Half the money goes to Population Control and Family Planning, the other half to wildlife conservation.) After the meeting I went to Lillywhites to get a wet-suit top for Phil. As I went down into the Underground I saw the headline 'Sadat Shot'. It was still unknown if he had been killed but as I drove home from Bristol

Mongolian Dotterel or
Mongolian Sand Plover
Charadrius mongolus

Wilson Island
16.10.81.

Heniochus
monocerus

Big Bommie

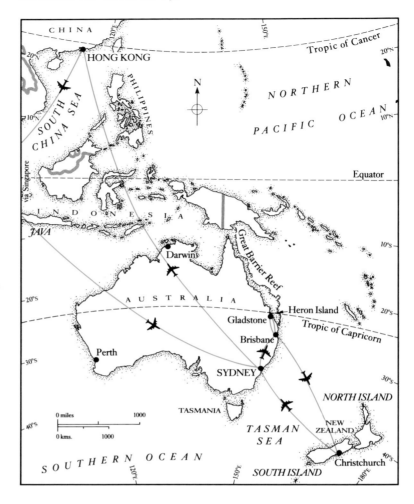

Parkway the 6 o'clock news confirmed that he had been. So all the plans for a Peace Park in Sinai may be back in the melting pot.

Today my day started with a line drawing of a stag and Golden Eagle for reproduction on the outside cover of some new water resisting notebooks which will be sold in our Wildfowl Trust shops. Then some corrections to my 'self portrait with Phil and other favourite animals', which is maybe three-quarters finished. Then I had to drive to Gloucester to get my new trifocal spectacles. Cassandra came with me so that we could work on the backlog of correspondence about the anti-whaling effort for 1982. In spite of all these preparations, a note from me for a Spanish book on the Antarctic had to be written out in my own hand thereby delaying our departure from 1600 to 1630. Then Phil and I set out for Gatwick Airport – a three-and-a-half hour journey. Our destination was the Gatwick Penta Hotel and bed after eating a small trout each.

THURSDAY 8 OCTOBER

We caught the bus to the airport and checked our five pieces (two containing diving gear) before going up to the Cathay Pacific Lounge. Although the complimentary tickets were Club Class they gave us First Class seats. From their VIP lounge I called Moira [Cuttell, then secretary] about no less than seven unresolved 'loose ends'.

Our journey was enriched after lunch because we followed the Anatolian coast and passed over the Greek out-post island of Castelhorizon which we visited 15 months ago with Louis Franck in the *Blue Albacor*. It was fascinating to see it from 25,000 ft.

We landed at Bahrain (a well known airport building to us after several transit visits) and then flew on, with Szechwan chicken for dinner, another bad movie, and an hour's sleep on the excellent new chaise-longue extensible seats, to a landing from the seaward end of the runway at Hong Kong where Nancy Nash met us and took us in a Hilton Mercedes to the Hong Kong Hilton. (It is now 9 October.) At the Hilton Philip Mormod (General Manager) was waiting to greet us and take us up to suite 1202 in which I have previously stayed. The Hong Kong Hilton has helped WWF in cash and kind to the tune of some 350,000 HK$ = £30,000. We went to bed soonest and slept through till 1700.

Then to a dinner in our honour given by Sir Kenneth Ping-Fan Fung, wife, two sons and a dozen businessmen and wives and Nancy, at the Nautilus club; all very well done and a superb dinner. I made a very short speech of thanks and Sir K replied.

SATURDAY 10 OCTOBER

Breakfast at 0900 and I woke Phil for no better reason than that her coffee would get cold. She could have slept an extra two hours and I felt very foolish as she really needed the sleep.

Lunch with our old friends John and Anne Marden. Later we flew on to Sydney via Singapore.

SUNDAY 11 OCTOBER

Arrived Sydney. We were met by Val Taylor. Driven by taxi in rain to their house in the suburb of Rosewall. Ron was there and we met Val's nephew – her brother's 17-year-old son called Mark Heighes (pronounced Hays) a nice looking lad with a mop of fair hair. He is to come with us to help with the diving gear.

The house is large with stained-glass windows and Victorian style architecture standing in a large garden which Val looks after, full of flowering shrubs and trees – very lovely in spite of the drizzling rain.

We had an hour or two at their home and then were off to the airport for a flight to Brisbane in a DC8 and a quick connection for a Fokker Friendship flight to Gladstone. (Brisbane Airport was very familiar as we slept some hours there in 1979.) Gladstone Airport

Cantherinus howensis
Filefish.

Moulted feathers
of the Bar-shouldered Dove
Geopelia humeralis

Heron Island from the air

was equally familiar and we had a quick transfer again to a five-seater helicopter for the 50-minute trip to Heron Island passing over Erskine Island. As we passed out to sea from the mainland I saw a large brown animal in the water, with its head above the water, which may have been a Leathery Turtle (Luth).

On the Erskine Reef I saw an Eagle Ray in the shallows which was probably *Aetobatis narinari*, and another on Wistari Reef as we came in to Heron.

Colin Lewis, the divemaster, took us to our rooms. We were in No. 55 in a cabin block called Coral Cay. The Taylors are in the next block. It was extremely nice to be back on the island – our fourth visit – after two years.

So for a delightful week we stayed at Heron, swimming morning and afternoon, re-remembering the fish fauna, listening at night to the crooning (or caterwauling, according to your taste) of the Wedge-tailed Shearwaters (*Puffinus pacificus*), and the ceaseless 'tek tek tekking' of the White-capped Noddies. We dived most days, though Phil had a tummy upset, which meant only three dives for her – but much snorkelling. On the morning of the last day we had a lovely dive together to 60 feet for 1 hour 10 minutes. Ron filmed us with a friendly Monocle Bream, *Scolopsis monogramma*, who came to feed when we turned over the sand, making a little cloud of sand.

Paraluteres prionurus. Filefish mimic of Toby.

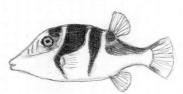

Filefish
Paraluteres prionurus

Toby
Canthigaster valentini.

Chelmon rostratus

Our next stop was for the main object of the whole journey. For five days we were in Christchurch, New Zealand for the IUCN General Assembly. Perhaps the most interesting discussions were about the conservation future of the Antarctic which promises to be a hot potato when the Antarctic Treaty comes up for renewal in 1990.

Mon 12th Oct a.m. Snorkelling S of the harbour entrance.
p.m. SCUBA in the harbour as a refresher course.

Sea Hare
Aplysia sp.
in the harbour.

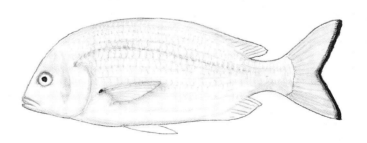

Acanthopagrus australis. Bream, or Brim.

When it came to the award of the John Phillips Medal a very nice thing happened. The President – my dear friend Professor Mohamed Kassas – invited me to make my acceptance speech. I was a little way into it when he rose and left the stage. At first I wondered whether this had anything to do with what I was saying, but he signalled me to go on. He then made his way down the aisle into the audience, took Philippa's hand, led her up on to the stage and sat her down next to him at the Presidential table. It was a characteristically generous gesture from one of the world's most brilliant and delightful conservationists.

While in Christchurch we paid a second visit to the new Antarctic wing of the National Museum which is absolutely first class, and went to see our old friend Dr David Harraway whose enthusiasm for Antarctic affairs is so heart-warming.

Scolopsis monogramma   c 40 cm.
The Gardens, Heron I.^s 18.10.81   60 ft

Macropharyngodon choati

Heron I^s 13.10.81   4 cm. and 10 cm.

White-capped Noddy Tern, *Anous minutus*, on Heron Island

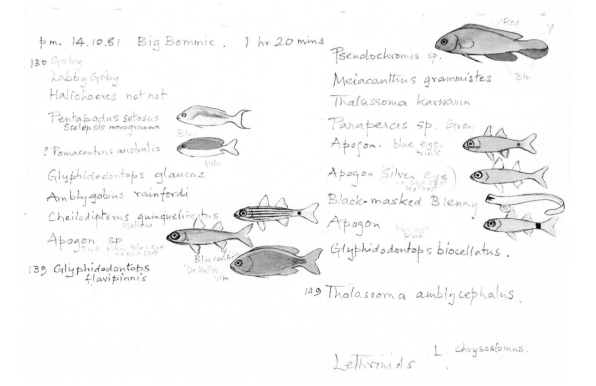

pm. 14.10.81   Big Bommie.   1 hr 20 mins

130 Goby

   Labby Goby

   Halichoeres not hot

   Pentapodus setosus
     Scolopsis monogramma

   ? Pomacentrus australis

   Glyphidodontops glaucus

   Amblygobius rainfordi

   Cheilodipterus quinquelineatus

   Apogon sp

139 Glyphidodontops
     flavipinnis

Psendochromis sp.

Meiacanthus grammistes

Thalassoma karwarin

Parapercis sp.

Apogon. blue eye.

Apogon (Silver eye)

Black-masked Blenny

Apogon

Glyphidodontops biocellatus.

149 Thalassoma amblycephalus.

Lethrinids   L. chrysostomus.

Precis sp.
? almana

FRIDAY 23 OCTOBER

Flight from Christchurch to Sydney. Met by Ron and Valerie (Taylor) and a herpetologist friend and film-maker whom I knew slightly – Thomas Schultze-Westrum. We were driven directly from the airport in the Taylor Range Rover 100 miles to the south west of Sydney, to Canyon Park – the home of Val's brother Greg Heighes (father of Mark who was with us at Heron Island). Tessie (Greg's wife) and 6-year-old Jonathon were there. The property is 1,900 acres of forest on both sides of a steep valley with the Kangaroo River running picturesquely down the middle. 150 cattle graze open grassland patches in the woodland.

We walked up a zigzag track watching and listening to birds like the lyre-bird, whip-bird, Golden Whistler etc and being shown by Thomas S-W two species of skink. Later we went down to the river, seeing a large Black Snake basking in the afternoon sun. It had a reddish belly and is extremely venomous. This was *Pseudechis porphyriacus*.

Greg drove us up to the farm where we saw Leseur's Water Lizard which did a splendid dive into a pool in a small stream we were crossing. We caught glimpses of two wallabies, a lyre-bird and an animal first identified as a wallaby, then as a wombat. As it retired under the trees at the edge of a 'paddock' I got the glasses on to it and saw spines. 'I think it's an echidna', I said, but no one would have it. 'No,' they all said, 'it was a baby wombat.' We walked over and found large wombat holes like a badger sett. Against a fallen tree bole, hidden in a dark crack, there was an echidna.

We had good views of a White-faced Heron and then went down a very steep hill with a narrow gap up which we had to return in the Range Rover. As it had slid most of the way down with no one in it, we all got out for the return climb, which was only accomplished at the third attempt.

There was talk of staying the night in the barn – where the Heighes family live in a caravan under the open barn roof. One end of the barn is enclosed to make a large living room with an open-ended floor above. But trying to make the four-hour drive back by

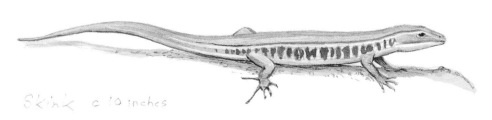

Skink c 10 inches

Smaller Skink
Emoia sp.

Birds from Sydney to the Kangaroo River.

Indian Mynah
Kurrawong.
Sulphur crested Cockatoo
Australian Crow
Grey Fantail
Silver Gull
European Starling
Cattle Egret
Australian Magpie
10 Spoonbill
House Sparrow
Little Pied Cormorant
Black Cormorant
Welcome Swallow
Kookaburra
Back Duck
Wonga Pigeon
Crimson Rosella
Wood Duck (Maned Goose)
20 White-faced Heron
Grey-breasted Silver-eye
Red-browed Finch
Superb Blue Wren
White winged Triller (♀) white rump
~~Lewin~~ Lewin Honeyeater
Large billed Scrub Wren
Lyre-bird
Whip-bird
Golden Whistler
30 Black faced Flycatcher
Rose Robin
Topknot Pigeon.
33. Southern Yellow Robin

(Nankeen Kestrel)

Walaby
Echidna
Wombat holes

Black Snake $3\frac{1}{2}$ / 4 ft long.

Leseurs Water Lizard
$2\frac{1}{2}$ feet long

Meadow Argus Butterfly
Precis villida calybe.

Grey.

Brick red

Brown

Crimson   grey

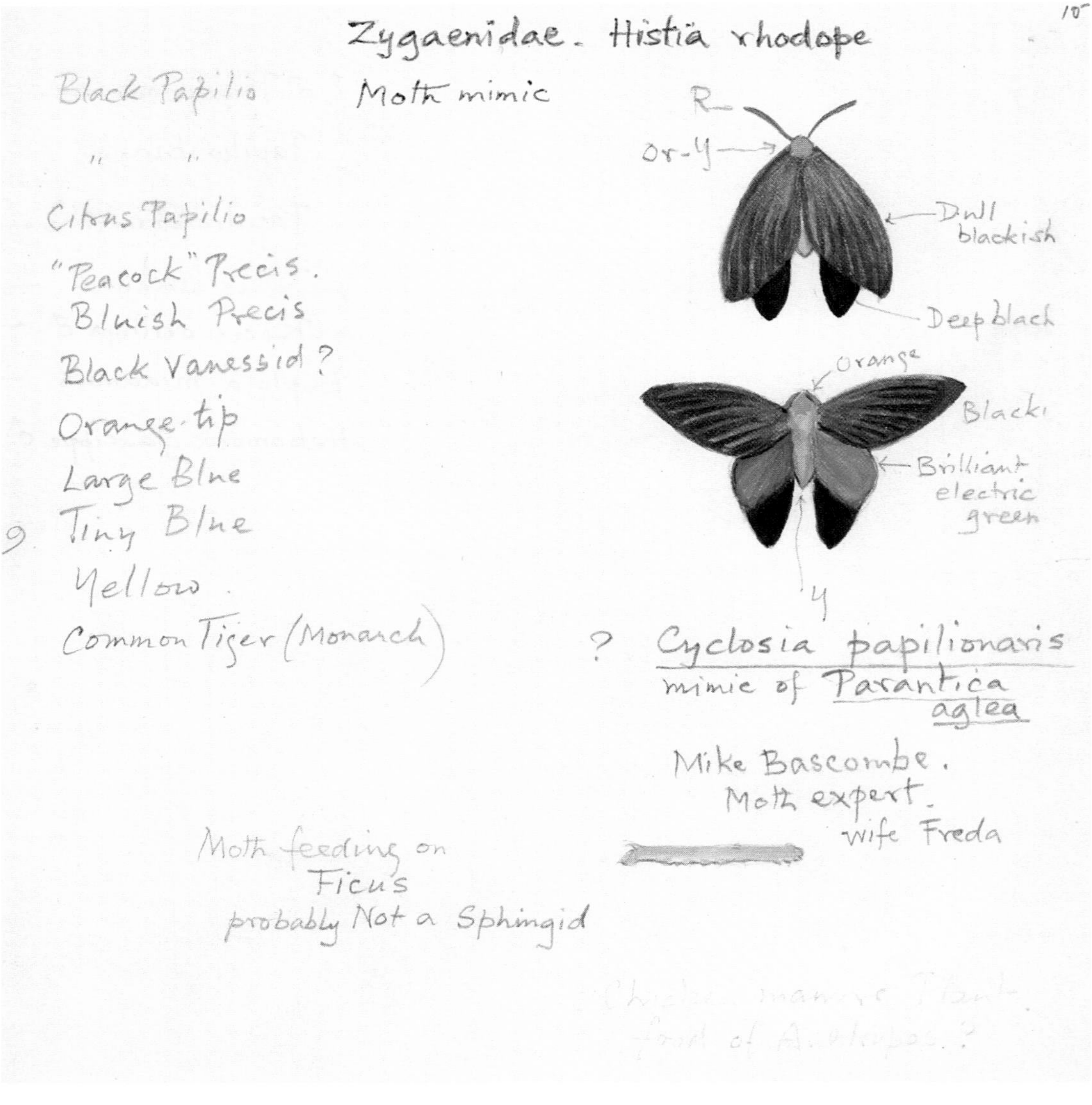
10
Zygaenidae. Histia rhodope
Moth mimic
Black Papilio
" "
Citrus Papilio
"Peacock" Precis.
Bluish Precis
Black Vanessid ?
Orange-tip
Large Blue
9 Tiny Blue
Yellow
Common Tiger (Monarch)
R
Or-Y
Dull blackish
Deep black
Orange
Black
Brilliant electric green
Y
? Cyclosia papilionaris
mimic of Parantica aglea
Mike Bascombe.
Moth expert.
wife Freda
Moth feeding on Ficus
probably Not a Sphingid

noon tomorrow was an unpromising prospect so we left at dusk. The journey took four and a half hours – after queuing for petrol because of a strike.

One of the high spots of the day had been 20 Australian Wood Ducks feeding in the grass 20 yards from the road, and a dozen more rather further away in another place. In each case there were a couple of pairs of Black Ducks (*Anas superciliosa*) too.

We liked Tessie very much and 6-year-old Jonathon was enchanting.

SATURDAY 24 OCTOBER
We flew from Sydney to Hong Kong where we were met by Ken and Sue Searle and taken to their apartment.

SUNDAY 25 OCTOBER
Quiet rest day at the Searles'. I counted 12 bird species and 11 butterfly species from their terrace.

MONDAY 26 OCTOBER
Mai Po Marshes. A fascinating day of birds and butterflies. We were guests of General John Chapple – a keen birder – who is anxious to develop Mai Po as a bird watching and educational amenity for the people of Hong Kong.

In a large RAF helicopter we went out from the helipad on the dockside of the Prince of Wales building to a football field north east of the Mai Po. There I was taken on a short flight round the marshes in a small chopper while Phil went by car.

The marshes have been reclaimed from a huge mud-fringed tidal bay by the building of a high bank to keep the sea out. Inside the 'sea wall' the great expanse of flat land – about five miles long and two wide – had been subdivided by low banks and water courses, largely for fish and shrimp culture. Outside the sea wall a substantial area is overgrown with a fairly dense mangrove forest. The shallow fresh, brackish and salt waters support an immense number and variety of water birds.

The Mai Po marshes

26.10.81. Maipo Marshes

Papilio polytes Common Mormon ♂

P. demolens
Lime Butterfly ♀
(Citrus Swallowtail)

P. paris
Paris Peacock ⟶ ♀

P. bianor ♂
Chinese
Peacock

Hypolimnas bolina
Great Eggfly ♀ ♂

Hypolimnas missipus
Danaid Eggfly ♂

Euploea midamus
Blue-spotted Crow ♂

Papilio memnon f. alcanor ♀
The Great Mormon.
ZBG Hong Kong. 27.10.81

Halcyon pileata
Black-capped
Kingfisher

Maipo Marshes
26.10.81.

The Wildfowl Trust is keen to assist in the development of the place as a much needed sanctuary – a Slimbridge-type operation on a very large scale, providing a huge educational potential, as well as a strong conservation element, and some considerable scientific value.

TUESDAY 27 OCTOBER
Our dear friend Joe Hotung gave an important lunch for me at the Hong Kong Club attended by Philip Kwok, of WWF/HK, (Prof) Brian Lofts, and David Akers-Jones, Secretary of the North West New Territories to whom I outlined my ideas for the Mai Po Marshes, which will be one of the major projects for WWF/HK. They will be able to use the techniques we have pioneered at Slimbridge and our other Wildfowl Trust centres for showing birds to people, and at the same time providing a safe sanctuary for them.

Danaus similis. Blue Glassy Tiger
or D. limniace. Blue Tiger
(blue)

Danaus chrysippus
Plain Tiger

Danaus genutia   Dark-veined Tiger

Graphium sarpedon
Common Bluebottle

♂

Graphium agamemnon
Tailed Green Jay

♂

Precis almana
Peacock Pansy

♂

Parathyma perius
Common Sergeant

♂

Papilio memnon
Great Mormon

form
alcanor ♀   ♂

WEDNESDAY 28 OCTOBER

At 1830 the Governor of Hong Kong, Sir Murray MacLehose, sent a car for me to 75 Peak Road (the Searle flat) and I had about half an hour at Government House. Although I had initiated the meeting, HE considered he had invited me to come and see him about the Mai Po Marshes Project.

He had been told that all the birds were in the northern part of Mai Po – belonging to the Communes from mainland China, and that the southern end which belongs to Hong Kong had few birds these days. I said I felt sure that if the habitat were manipulated the birds would come to any part of the marshes.

I reported that the Secretary for the New Territories, David Akers-Jones, whom I had met yesterday, was in favour of the project as was also the Director of the Department of Agriculture and Fisheries, John Ridell Swan, who had spent Monday morning with us on the marshes.

HE was concerned about cost – eg extension of access road, Nature Centre, hides, fences etc. I said I thought WWF/HK might contribute and stressed the educational value if it is well done.

When I left, his attitude seemed quite positive. WWF/HK will fund an expert from the Wildfowl Trust to come out soonest to draw up plans for the Mai Po Nature Reserve, Bird Observatory and Education Centre.

THURSDAY 29 OCTOBER

We have had five pretty strenuous days in Hong Kong, based at Ken and Sue Searle's flat on the ground floor of No. 75 Peak Road – part of a Hotung mansion. The elderly Hotung who lives in the rest of the house is related to our friend Joe Hotung, but they are not on good terms!

The Searle home consisted of high rooms – a sitting room, a dining room, two large bedrooms (theirs and ours) each with bathroom beyond. In the small hall leading to the kitchen was a large aquarium teeming with Neon Tetras etc, which had been full of salt water until a week before.

Our bedroom housed the main library of zoology with most of the books leather-bound in dark blue. It was an excellent reference library for bird and mammal books.

About the most delightful feature of the flat, inside, was the impeccable taste of the pictures, rugs and *objets d'art*, including a superb Hahn horse. No less wonderful was the view from the terrace where we had breakfast each day with a breathtaking view over the sea hundreds of feet below – softened while we were there by a haze through which the harbour of Aberdeen, with its massed sampans at the foot of the steep slope, looked positively romantic.

The porch with breakfast table and *Ficus* tree (somewhat damaged by the larvae of a moth) gave way down a flight of steps to a large grass terrace with a balustrade and a small pavilion at the corner.

Phragmites in the Mai Po marshes.

The lawn, although given much attention by gardeners, was not very green. The terrace was the territory of the landlord, but we were able to use it for bird and butterfly watching in the steep gully below and to the left, where the watered vegetable garden and a canalized water-course attracted Grey Wagtails and a large number of dragonflies and butterflies. Kites in numbers used the hill lift for soaring.

We were sad to leave Hong Kong and the warm hospitality of Ken and Sue Searle, but the Mai Po interlude has been enormously interesting and enjoyable and my introduction to the lepidoptery of eastern China especially stimulating.

217

Hebomoia glaucippe
The Great Orangetip.

Postscript, 1986. The Mai Po project is well advanced in its development and shows every chance of becoming a successful show-place for conservation as well as a vital link in the migratory chain along the West Pacific flyway.

An interesting side-effect, not foreseen at the time the project began, is that the Chinese Government, not to be outdone, is apparently declaring an even larger area on the Chinese side of the bay as a reserve under full protection.

This could mean that the future of Mai Po will extend into the 21st century.

Index

Numbers in italics refer to captions